An Nasihah

Islamic Curriculum

Sūrah & Du`ā’

…lete
Syllabus

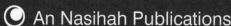

An Nasihah Publications

Every effort has been made to ensure the correctness of the content. The publishers will gladly receive information enabling them to rectify any error or omission in subsequent editions.

First Edition March 2016
Second Edition July 2016

An Nasihah Publications Ltd.
114 Harborough Road
Leicester LE2 4LD
United Kingdom

www.an-nasihah.com
admin@an-nasihah.com

Distributors in the UK: Azhar Academy, London
www.azharacademy.com

British Library Cataloguing in Publication Data
A catalogue record for this book is available from the British Library.

Name: ______________________________

Class: ______________________________

Introduction

All praises are due to Allah سبحانه وتعالى, Lord of the heavens and earth. May Peace and blessings be upon our Noble Messenger, Muḥammad صلى الله عليه وسلم.

Together with the eight coursebooks and their corresponding workbooks, this unique Surah and Du'ā' book is being published with the grace of Allāh سبحانه وتعالى. It contains all the sūrah and du'ā's a Muslim needs in his/her day-to-day life.

Each section has been arranged according to the age and ability of the child.

F1 & F2 - represents Foundation 1 and Foundation 2 (The first two years of madrasah). In these years pupils will not be studying a book but will be required to learn a few sūrah and some du'ā's.

Thereafter pupils will be required to learn the respective du'ā'sand sūrahs according to their coursebook year. If a pupil completes all the assigned memorisation for that year he/she should try to learn the meaning and keep re-visiting them.

Introduction

A box has been allocated for the teachers to mark the pupil's errors under each line of sūrah or du'ā'.
Once a sūrah or du'ā' is completed, the teacher will sign and date the box provided or advise the student to repeat it by tracing the 'R' symbol.

A revision tracker has been placed towards the end of the book wherein a list of all the sūrah and du'ā' have been written. This tracker may be used at the beginning of every year or whenever the teacher feels the need. This will assist in ensuring that the sūrahs and du'ā's are constantly revisited.

I pray Allah سبحانه وتعالى accepts this humble work in His court, rewards all those who were part of this publication in anyway, their families and their associates with His pleasure and success in both the worlds. Āmīn.

If you find any fault, then correct it I pray,
for no one is faultless except Allāh Ta'āla
(Jalāl-ud-dīn Suyūti)

Shaykh Muḥammad Yaḥyā
Director, An Nasihah Publications

Rajab 1436/May 2015

Syllabus

Coursebook:	F1	F2
Age Range:	4-5 yrs	5-6 yrs
Sūrah	1. Fātiḥah	1. An Nās 2. Al Falaq 3. Al Ikhlāṣ
Du'ā'	1. 1st Kalimah 2. Before starting something 3. Ta'awwudh 4. Du'ā' for eating 5. Du'ā' for sleeping 6. Greeting a Muslim 7. Replying to a Muslim's greeting 8. Before drinking water 9. After drinking water	1. 2nd Kalimah - Shahādah 2. 3rd Kalimah 3. Du'ā' when sneezing and replying to it 4. Du'ā' when thanking someone 5. Making intention to do something 6. Du'ā' when seeing a Muslim happy 7. Du'ā' when entering the toilet 8. Du'ā' when exiting the toilet 9. After eating 10. Du'ā' if one forgets to recite the name of Allāh Ta'āla before eating 11. Du'ā' after drinking milk 12. After waking up
Names of Allāh	5 names of Allāh	5 names of Allāh

C1	C2	C3
6-7 yrs	7-8 yrs	8-9 yrs
1. Al Lahab 2. An Naṣr 3. Al Kāfirūn	1. Al Kawthar 2. Al Ma'ūn 3. Quraysh 4. Al Fīl 5. Al Humazah	1. Al 'Aṣr 2. At Takāthur 3. Al Qāri'ah 4. Al 'Ādiyāt 5. Az Zalzalah
1. 4th Kalimah 2. 5th Kalimah 3. Takbīr 4. Tasbīḥ of rukū' 5. After rukū' 6. During qawmah 7. Tasbīḥ in sujūd 8. During jalsa 9. To end ṣalāh by making salām 10. Thanā 11. To increase one's knowledge 12. When climbing 13. When descending	1. Imān Mujmal 2. Imān Mufaṣṣal 3. Tashahhud 4. Salawāt (Durūd Ibrāhīm) 5. Du'ā' before salām 6. Du'ā' after ṣalāh 7. Du'ā' before wuḍū' 8. During wuḍū' 9. After wuḍū' 10. Du'ā' when entering the masjid 11. Du'ā' when exiting the masjid 12. Du'ā' after ṣalāh	1. When you see someone smiling 2. Du'ā' for parents 3. Asking Allāh Ta'āla for forgiveness (After Fajr, 'Asr and before sleeping) 4. Du'ā' when leaving and entering the house 5. Qunūt 6. When wearing and taking off clothes 7. Du'ā' to a host 8. When breaking fast 9. After Iftār 10. Making Iftār at someone's place 11. When travelling in a vehicle 12. When it's raining 13. When looking in the mirror
10 names of Allāh	10 names of Allāh	10 names of Allāh

Syllabus

Coursebook:	C4	C5
Age Range:	9-10 yrs	10-11 yrs
Sūrah	1. Al Bayyinah 2. Al Qadr 3. Al 'Alaq 4. At Ṭīn	1. Al Inshirāḥ 2. Ad Dhuḥā 3. Last 2 Āyāt of Sūrah Al-Baqarah
Du'ā'	1. Ayatul Kursi 2. Du'ā' for someone you hold dear 3. Replying to the person who expresses their love 4. Adhān 5. Replying to the Adhān 6. Iqāmah 7. Replying to the Iqāmah 8. Du'ā' after Adhān 9. Janāzah du'ā' 10. Janāzah du'ā' for infants 11. Du'ā' when hearing a dog barking in the night 12. After drinking Zamzam water	1. Protection from all calamities 2. Du'ā' for Laylatul Qadr 3. On seeing a new moon 4. Du'ā' at the end of a gathering 5. When feeling pain 6. When visiting a sick person, asking Allāh Ta'āla for cure 7. When a loss or difficulty occurs 8. When angry 9. Being pleased with Islām 10. Giving Du'ā' of blessings 11. Du'ā' after ṣalāh of need
99 Names of Allāh	15 names of Allāh	15 names of Allāh

C6	C7	C8
11-12 yrs	12-13 yrs	13-14 yrs
1. 1st 10 Āyāt Sūrah Al-Kahf 2. Last 2 Āyāt of Surah Hashr 3. Sūrah Yāsīn - 3 Rukū'	1. Sūrah Yāsīn – Full 2. Sūrah Sajdah	1. Sūrah Mulk 2. Sūrah Waqi'ah
1. Removing doubts 2. When embarking on a journey 3. When returning from a journey 4. Saying farewell 5. Wearing new clothes 6. When you see someone wearing new clothes 7. Protection from evil eye, harmful creatures and Shayṭān 8. Morning and evening Du'ā's 9. When in the market place 10. When lying down to sleep 11. On seeing dreams 12. What to read upon waking up during the night 13. Remove fear before sleeping or after nightmare 14. When intending to enter a town or city	1. Du'ā' of all du'ā's - The Prophet's comprehensive Du'ā' 2. When you see someone afflicted or suffering 3. Talbiyah 4. Takbīr of Tashrīq 5. When the sun rises 6. When there is excessive downpour 7. When one's gaze falls on the moon 8. When you hear thunder 9. When visiting the graveyard 10. At the time of death 11. At the time of burying the deceased 12. When filling the qabr with soil 13. When you experience solar or lunar eclipse	1. Sayyidul Istigfār 2. Du'ā' for seeking guidance – Istikhārah Du'ā' 3. Qunūt Nāzilah 4. Du'ā' to remove worry and sorrow 5. Before slaughtering an animal 6. Du'ā' for difficult tasks 7. Asking for rain 8. When seeing the first fruits of the season 9. Du'ā's from the Qur'ān and Ḥadīth
15 names of Allāh	14 names of Allāh	99 names of Allāh

الْحَمْدُ لِلَّهِ رَبِّ الْعَالَمِينَ
وَالصَّلَاةُ وَالسَّلَامُ عَلَىٰ نَبِيِّنَا مُحَمَّدٍ
وَعَلَىٰ آلِهِ وَصَحْبِهِ أَجْمَعِينَ

بِسْمِ اللهِ الرَّحْمٰنِ الرَّحِيمِ

CONTENTS PAGE

F1
SŪRAH

Sūrah Al-Fātiḥa

بِسۡمِ اللّٰهِ الرَّحۡمٰنِ الرَّحِيۡمِ

In the name of Allāh, the Beneficent,
the Merciful.

اَلۡحَمۡدُ لِلّٰهِ رَبِّ الۡعٰلَمِيۡنَ ۙ‏ ﴿۱﴾

Praise belongs to Allāh, the Lord of all the worlds.

الرَّحۡمٰنِ الرَّحِيۡمِ ۙ‏ ﴿۲﴾

The All-Merciful, the Very-Merciful.

مٰلِكِ يَوۡمِ الدِّيۡنِ ؕ‏ ﴿۳﴾

The Master of the Day of Judgement.

DATE:	✓	R

Sūrah Al-Fātiḥa

إِيَّاكَ نَعْبُدُ وَإِيَّاكَ نَسْتَعِينُ ﴿٤﴾

You alone do we worship, and from You alone do we seek help.

اِهْدِنَا الصِّرَاطَ الْمُسْتَقِيمَ ﴿٥﴾

Guide us to the straight path

صِرَاطَ الَّذِينَ أَنْعَمْتَ عَلَيْهِمْ ۙ

غَيْرِ الْمَغْضُوبِ عَلَيْهِمْ وَلَا الضَّالِّينَ ﴿٧﴾

The path of those upon whom You have bestowed Your Grace, not of those who have evoked (Your) anger or of those who are astray.

DATE:	✓	R

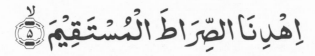

F2
SŪRAH

Sūrah An-Nās

بِسۡمِ اللّٰهِ الرَّحۡمٰنِ الرَّحِيۡمِ

In the name of Allāh, the Beneficent, the Merciful.

قُلۡ اَعُوۡذُ بِرَبِّ النَّاسِۙ ۝١

Say, "I seek refuge in the Lord of mankind,

مَلِكِ النَّاسِۙ ۝٢

The King of mankind,

اِلٰهِ النَّاسِۙ ۝٣

The God of mankind,

DATE:	✓	R

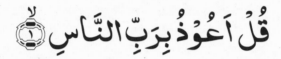

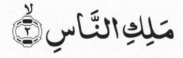

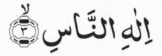

Sūrah An-Nās

مِن شَرِّ الْوَسْوَاسِ الْخَنَّاسِ ٤

From the evil of the retreating whisperer,

الَّذِي يُوَسْوِسُ فِي صُدُورِ النَّاسِ ٥

The one who whispers in the hearts of people,

مِنَ الْجِنَّةِ وَالنَّاسِ ٦

From among the jinn and mankind."

DATE:	✓	R

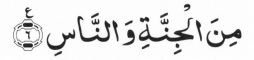

Sūrah Al-Falaq

بِسۡمِ اللّٰهِ الرَّحۡمٰنِ الرَّحِيۡمِ

In the name of Allāh, the Beneficent, the Merciful.

قُلۡ اَعُوۡذُ بِرَبِّ الۡفَلَقِۙ ﴿۱﴾

Say, "I seek refuge with the Lord of the daybreak

مِنۡ شَرِّ مَا خَلَقَۙ ﴿۲﴾

From the evil of everything He has created,

وَمِنۡ شَرِّ غَاسِقٍ اِذَا وَقَبَۙ ﴿۳﴾

And from the evil of darkness when it settles,

وَمِنۡ شَرِّ النَّفّٰثٰتِ فِى الۡعُقَدِۙ ﴿۴﴾

And from the evil of the women who blow on the knots,

وَمِنۡ شَرِّ حَاسِدٍ اِذَا حَسَدَ ﴿۵﴾

And from the evil of an envier when he envies."

DATE:	✓	R

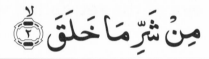

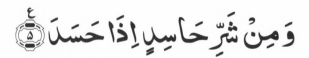

Sūrah Al-Ikhlāṣ

بِسۡمِ اللّٰهِ الرَّحۡمٰنِ الرَّحِيۡمِ

In the name of Allāh, the Beneficent, the Merciful.

قُلۡ هُوَ اللّٰهُ اَحَدٌ ۚ‏ ﴿۱﴾

Say, "He is Allāh , (who is) One,

اَللّٰهُ الصَّمَدُ ۚ‏ ﴿۲﴾

Allāh, the Independent.

لَمۡ يَلِدۡ ۙ وَلَمۡ يُوۡلَدۡ ۙ‏ ﴿۳﴾

He neither gives birth nor is born,

وَلَمۡ يَكُنۡ لَّهٗ كُفُوًا اَحَدٌ ‏ ﴿۴﴾

And there is no one equal to Him."

DATE:	✓	R

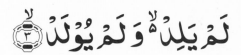

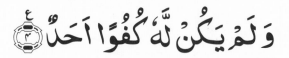

C1
SŪRAH

Sūrah Al-Lahab

بِسۡمِ اللّٰهِ الرَّحۡمٰنِ الرَّحِیۡمِ

In the name of Allāh, the Beneficent, the Merciful.

تَبَّتۡ یَدَاۤ اَبِیۡ لَهَبٍ وَّ تَبَّ ﴿۱﴾

May the hands of Abū Lahab be ruined, and ruined is he.

مَاۤ اَغۡنٰی عَنۡهُ مَالُهٗ وَ مَا كَسَبَ ﴿۲﴾

Neither his wealth benefited him, nor what he earned.

سَیَصۡلٰی نَارًا ذَاتَ لَهَبٍ ﴿۳﴾

He will soon enter a Fire, full of flames,

وَّ امۡرَاَتُهٗ ؕ حَمَّالَةَ الۡحَطَبِ ﴿۴﴾

And his wife (as well) - the carrier of firewood.

فِیۡ جِیۡدِهَا حَبۡلٌ مِّنۡ مَّسَدٍ ﴿۵﴾

Around her neck is a rope of (twisted) fibre.

DATE:	✓	R

Sūrah An-Naṣr

بِسۡمِ اللّٰهِ الرَّحۡمٰنِ الرَّحِيۡمِ

In the name of Allāh, the Beneficent, the Merciful.

اِذَا جَآءَ نَصۡرُ اللّٰهِ وَالۡفَتۡحُ ۙ﴿۱﴾

When Allāh's help and victory comes,

وَرَاَيۡتَ النَّاسَ يَدۡخُلُوۡنَ فِىۡ دِيۡنِ اللّٰهِ اَفۡوَاجًا ۙ﴿۲﴾

And you see the people entering into the religion of Allāh in crowds,

فَسَبِّحۡ بِحَمۡدِ رَبِّكَ وَاسۡتَغۡفِرۡهُ ؕ

Then glorify (Him) with praise of your Lord and ask forgiveness of Him.

اِنَّهٗ كَانَ تَوَّابًا ﴿۳﴾

Indeed, He is ever accepting of repentance.

DATE:	✓	R

Sūrah Al-Kāfirūn

بِسۡمِ اللّٰهِ الرَّحۡمٰنِ الرَّحِيۡمِ

In the name of Allāh, the Beneficent, the Merciful.

قُلۡ يٰۤاَيُّهَا الۡكٰفِرُوۡنَ ۙ﴿١﴾

Say, "O disbelievers,

لَاۤ اَعۡبُدُ مَا تَعۡبُدُوۡنَ ۙ﴿٢﴾

I do not worship what you worship.

وَلَاۤ اَنۡتُمۡ عٰبِدُوۡنَ مَاۤ اَعۡبُدُ ۚ﴿٣﴾

Nor are you worshippers of what I worship.

وَلَاۤ اَنَا عَابِدٌ مَّا عَبَدۡتُّمۡ ۙ﴿٤﴾

Nor will I be a worshipper of what you worship.

وَلَاۤ اَنۡتُمۡ عٰبِدُوۡنَ مَاۤ اَعۡبُدُ ؕ﴿٥﴾

Nor will you be worshippers of what I worship.

لَكُمۡ دِيۡنُكُمۡ وَلِيَ دِيۡنِ ﴿٦﴾

For you is your religion, and for me is my religion.

DATE:	✓	R

C2
SŪRAH

Sūrah Al-Kauthar

بِسْمِ اللّٰهِ الرَّحْمٰنِ الرَّحِيْمِ

In the name of Allāh, the Beneficent, the Merciful.

اِنَّآ اَعْطَيْنٰكَ الْكَوْثَرَ ۝١

Indeed, We have granted you, (O Muḥammad), al-Kawthar.

فَصَلِّ لِرَبِّكَ وَانْحَرْ ۝٢

So pray to your Lord and sacrifice.

اِنَّ شَانِئَكَ هُوَ الْاَبْتَرُ ۝٣

Indeed, your enemy is the one cut off (from all good).

DATE:	✓	R

Sūrah Al-Mā'ūn

بِسْمِ اللّٰهِ الرَّحْمٰنِ الرَّحِيْمِ

In the name of Allāh, the Beneficent, the Merciful.

اَرَءَيْتَ الَّذِيْ يُكَذِّبُ بِالدِّيْنِ ﴿١﴾

Have you seen the one who denies the Day of Judgement?

فَذٰلِكَ الَّذِيْ يَدُعُّ الْيَتِيْمَ ﴿٢﴾

So, he is the one who pushes away the orphan,

وَلَا يَحُضُّ عَلٰى طَعَامِ الْمِسْكِيْنِ ﴿٣﴾

And does not encourage the feeding of the poor.

فَوَيْلٌ لِّلْمُصَلِّيْنَ ﴿٤﴾

So woe to those who pray,

الَّذِيْنَ هُمْ عَنْ صَلَاتِهِمْ سَاهُوْنَ ﴿٥﴾

(But) who are heedless of their prayer,

الَّذِيْنَ هُمْ يُرَآءُوْنَ ﴿٦﴾

Who (do good only to) show off,

وَيَمْنَعُوْنَ الْمَاعُوْنَ ﴿٧﴾

And refuse (to give even) small gifts.

DATE:	✓	R

Sūrah Quraish

بِسۡمِ اللّٰهِ الرَّحۡمٰنِ الرَّحِيۡمِ

In the name of Allāh, the Beneficent,
the Merciful.

لِاِيۡلٰفِ قُرَيۡشٍۙ ﴿۱﴾

Because of the familiarity of the Quraish,

اٖلٰفِهِمۡ رِحۡلَةَ الشِّتَآءِ وَالصَّيۡفِۚ ﴿۲﴾

That is, their familiarity with the trips of winter and summer,

فَلۡيَعۡبُدُوۡا رَبَّ هٰذَا الۡبَيۡتِۙ ﴿۳﴾

Let them worship the Lord of this House,

الَّذِىۡۤ اَطۡعَمَهُمۡ مِّنۡ جُوۡعٍ ۙ وَّاٰمَنَهُمۡ مِّنۡ خَوۡفٍ ﴿۴﴾

Who gave them food against hunger, and gave them security against fear.

DATE:	✓	R

Sūrah Al-Fīl

بِسۡمِ اللّٰہِ الرَّحۡمٰنِ الرَّحِیۡمِ

In the name of Allāh, the Beneficent, the Merciful.

اَلَمۡ تَرَ کَیۡفَ فَعَلَ رَبُّکَ بِاَصۡحٰبِ الۡفِیۡلِ ﴿۱﴾

Have you not considered, (O Muḥammad), how your Lord dealt with the People of the Elephant?

اَلَمۡ یَجۡعَلۡ کَیۡدَہُمۡ فِیۡ تَضۡلِیۡلٍ ﴿۲﴾

Did He not make their plan into misguidance?

وَّ اَرۡسَلَ عَلَیۡہِمۡ طَیۡرًا اَبَابِیۡلَ ﴿۳﴾

And He sent against them birds in flocks,

تَرۡمِیۡہِمۡ بِحِجَارَۃٍ مِّنۡ سِجِّیۡلٍ ﴿۴﴾

Striking them with stones of hard clay,

فَجَعَلَہُمۡ کَعَصۡفٍ مَّاۡکُوۡلٍ ﴿۵﴾

And He made them like eaten straw.

DATE:	✓	R

Sūrah Al-Humazah

بِسۡمِ اللّٰهِ الرَّحۡمٰنِ الرَّحِيۡمِ

In the name of Allāh, the Beneficent,
the Merciful.

وَيۡلٌ لِّكُلِّ هُمَزَةٍ لُّمَزَةِ ۙ ﴿١﴾

Woe to every backbiter and slanderer.

الَّذِىۡ جَمَعَ مَالًا وَّعَدَّدَهٗ ۙ ﴿٢﴾

Who collects wealth and (continuously) counts it.

يَحۡسَبُ اَنَّ مَالَهٗۤ اَخۡلَدَهٗ ۚ ﴿٣﴾

He thinks that his wealth will make him eternal.

كَلَّا لَيُنۡۢبَذَنَّ فِى الۡحُطَمَةِ ۖ ﴿٤﴾

No! He will surely be thrown into the Crushing Fire.

DATE:	✓	R

Sūrah Al-Humazah

وَمَآ أَدۡرَىٰكَ مَا ٱلۡحُطَمَةُ ٥

And what may let you know what the Crushing Fire is?

نَارُ ٱللَّهِ ٱلۡمُوقَدَةُ ٦

It is Allāh's kindled fire

ٱلَّتِي تَطَّلِعُ عَلَى ٱلۡأَفۡـِٔدَةِ ٧

That will peep into the hearts.

إِنَّهَا عَلَيۡهِم مُّؤۡصَدَةٞ ٨

Indeed, it (Hellfire) will be closed down upon them

فِي عَمَدٖ مُّمَدَّدَةِۭ ٩

In extended columns.

DATE:	✓	R

C3
SŪRAH

Sūrah Al-Asr

بِسۡمِ اللّٰهِ الرَّحۡمٰنِ الرَّحِيۡمِ

In the name of Allāh, the Beneficent, the Merciful.

وَالۡعَصۡرِۙ ﴿۱﴾

(I take an oath) by Time,

اِنَّ الۡاِنۡسَانَ لَفِىۡ خُسۡرٍۙ ﴿۲﴾

Indeed, mankind is in loss,

اِلَّا الَّذِيۡنَ اٰمَنُوۡا وَعَمِلُوا الصّٰلِحٰتِ وَتَوَاصَوۡا بِالۡحَقِّ ۙ۬

وَتَوَاصَوۡا بِالصَّبۡرِ ﴿۳﴾

Except for those who have believed and did righteous deeds and advised each other to follow truth and advised each other to observe patience.

DATE: | ✓ | R

Sūrah At-Takāthur

بِسْمِ اللهِ الرَّحْمٰنِ الرَّحِيْمِ

In the name of Allāh, the Beneficent, the Merciful.

اَلْهٰكُمُ التَّكَاثُرُ ﴿١﴾

You are distracted by competition in increasing (worldly benefits),

حَتّٰى زُرْتُمُ الْمَقَابِرَ ﴿٢﴾

Until you visit the graveyards.

كَلَّا سَوْفَ تَعْلَمُوْنَ ﴿٣﴾

No! You will soon know.

ثُمَّ كَلَّا سَوْفَ تَعْلَمُوْنَ ﴿٤﴾

Again, you will soon know.

DATE:	✓	R

Sūrah At-Takāthur

كَلَّا لَوْ تَعْلَمُونَ عِلْمَ الْيَقِينِ ﴿٥﴾

No! If you only knew with knowledge of certainty...

لَتَرَوُنَّ الْجَحِيمَ ﴿٦﴾

You will surely see the Hellfire.

ثُمَّ لَتَرَوُنَّهَا عَيْنَ الْيَقِينِ ﴿٧﴾

Then you will surely see it with the eye of certainty.

ثُمَّ لَتُسْـَٔلُنَّ يَوْمَئِذٍ عَنِ النَّعِيمِ ﴿٨﴾

Then you will be asked about all the pleasures (you enjoyed in the world).

DATE:	✓	R

Sūrah Al-Qāri'ah

بِسْمِ اللّٰهِ الرَّحْمٰنِ الرَّحِيْمِ

In the name of Allāh, the Beneficent, the Merciful.

اَلْقَارِعَةُ ﴿١﴾

The Striking Calamity

مَا الْقَارِعَةُ ﴿٢﴾

What is the Striking Calamity?

وَمَآ اَدْرٰىكَ مَا الْقَارِعَةُ ﴿٣﴾

And what may let you know what the Striking Calamity is?

يَوْمَ يَكُوْنُ النَّاسُ كَالْفَرَاشِ الْمَبْثُوْثِ ﴿٤﴾

(It will happen) on a day when people will be like scattered moths.

وَتَكُوْنُ الْجِبَالُ كَالْعِهْنِ الْمَنْفُوْشِ ﴿٥﴾

And the mountains will be like wool, fluffed up.

فَاَمَّا مَنْ ثَقُلَتْ مَوَازِيْنُهٗ ﴿٦﴾

Then as for him whose scales are heavy (with good deeds),

Sūrah Al-Qāri'ah

فَهُوَ فِي عِيشَةٍ رَّاضِيَةٍ ﴿٧﴾

He will be in a pleasant life.

وَأَمَّا مَنْ خَفَّتْ مَوَازِينُهُ ﴿٨﴾

But as for him whose scales are light,

فَأُمُّهُ هَاوِيَةٌ ﴿٩﴾

His abode will be an abyss.

وَمَا أَدْرَاكَ مَا هِيَهْ ﴿١٠﴾

And what can make you know what that is?

نَارٌ حَامِيَةٌ ﴿١١﴾

A blazing Fire!

DATE:	✓	R

Sūrah Al-'Ādiyāt

بِسْمِ اللّٰهِ الرَّحْمٰنِ الرَّحِيْمِ

In the name of Allāh, the Beneficent, the Merciful.

وَالْعٰدِيٰتِ ضَبْحًا ۙ﴿١﴾

(I take an oath) by those (horses) that run snorting,

فَالْمُوْرِيٰتِ قَدْحًا ۙ﴿٢﴾

Then those that create sparks by striking (their hoofs) on the stones

فَالْمُغِيْرٰتِ صُبْحًا ۙ﴿٣﴾

Then those that invade at morning,

فَاَثَرْنَ بِهٖ نَقْعًا ۙ﴿٤﴾

Then raise, at the same time, a trail of dust,

فَوَسَطْنَ بِهٖ جَمْعًا ۙ﴿٥﴾

Arriving thereby in the center collectively,

اِنَّ الْاِنْسَانَ لِرَبِّهٖ لَكَنُوْدٌ ۚ﴿٦﴾

Indeed mankind, to his Lord, is ungrateful.

DATE:	✓	R

Sūrah Al-'Ādiyāt

وَإِنَّهُۥ عَلَىٰ ذَٰلِكَ لَشَهِيدٌ ۝٧

And he himself is a witness to that fact,

وَإِنَّهُۥ لِحُبِّ ٱلْخَيْرِ لَشَدِيدٌ ۝٨

And in his love for wealth, he is very intense.

۞ أَفَلَا يَعْلَمُ إِذَا بُعْثِرَ مَا فِى ٱلْقُبُورِ ۝٩

But does he not know that when the contents of the graves are scattered,

وَحُصِّلَ مَا فِى ٱلصُّدُورِ ۝١٠

And all that is contained in the hearts will be exposed:

إِنَّ رَبَّهُم بِهِمْ يَوْمَئِذٍ لَّخَبِيرٌۢ ۝١١

Surely your Lord, that day, is fully aware of them.

DATE:	✓	R

Sūrah Az-Zalzalah

بِسْمِ اللّٰهِ الرَّحْمٰنِ الرَّحِيْمِ

In the name of Allāh, the Beneficent,
the Merciful.

اِذَا زُلْزِلَتِ الْاَرْضُ زِلْزَالَهَا ۙ﴿۱﴾

When the Earth is shaken with its earthquake

وَاَخْرَجَتِ الْاَرْضُ اَثْقَالَهَا ۙ﴿۲﴾

And when the Earth throws out its burdens,

وَقَالَ الْاِنْسَانُ مَا لَهَا ۚ﴿۳﴾

And man says, "What is (wrong) with it?" -

يَوْمَئِذٍ تُحَدِّثُ اَخْبَارَهَا ۙ﴿۴﴾

That day, it will report its news

DATE:	✓	R

Sūrah Az-Zalzalah

بِأَنَّ رَبَّكَ أَوْحَىٰ لَهَا ٥

Because your Lord has commanded it.

يَوْمَئِذٍ يَصْدُرُ النَّاسُ أَشْتَاتًا لِّيُرَوْا أَعْمَالَهُمْ ٦

That day the people will come back in different groups, so that they may be shown their deeds.

فَمَن يَعْمَلْ مِثْقَالَ ذَرَّةٍ خَيْرًا يَرَهُ ٧

So whoever does an atom's weight of good will see it,

وَمَن يَعْمَلْ مِثْقَالَ ذَرَّةٍ شَرًّا يَرَهُ ٨

And whoever does an atom's weight of evil will see it.

DATE:	✓	R

C4
SŪRAH

Sūrah Al-Bayyinah

بِسْمِ اللّٰهِ الرَّحْمٰنِ الرَّحِيْمِ

In the name of Allāh, the Beneficent, the Merciful.

لَمْ يَكُنِ الَّذِيْنَ كَفَرُوْا مِنْ اَهْلِ الْكِتٰبِ وَالْمُشْرِكِيْنَ مُنْفَكِّيْنَ حَتّٰى تَاْتِيَهُمُ الْبَيِّنَةُ ﴿١﴾

Those who disbelieved from among the People of the Book and the polytheists were not (expected) to abstain (from their wrong beliefs) unless a clear proof comes to them,

رَسُوْلٌ مِّنَ اللّٰهِ يَتْلُوْا صُحُفًا مُّطَهَّرَةً ﴿٢﴾

A Messenger from Allāh, reciting purified scriptures

فِيْهَا كُتُبٌ قَيِّمَةٌ ﴿٣﴾

Within which are correct writings.

وَمَا تَفَرَّقَ الَّذِيْنَ اُوْتُوا الْكِتٰبَ اِلَّا مِنْ بَعْدِ مَا جَآءَتْهُمُ الْبَيِّنَةُ ﴿٤﴾

And those who were given the Book did not disagree but after the clear proof came to them,

وَمَآ اُمِرُوْٓا اِلَّا لِيَعْبُدُوا اللّٰهَ مُخْلِصِيْنَ لَهُ الدِّيْنَ ۙ حُنَفَآءَ وَيُقِيْمُوا الصَّلٰوةَ وَيُؤْتُوا الزَّكٰوةَ

And they were not commanded except to worship Allāh, (being) sincere to Him in religion, inclining to truth, and to establish prayer and to give zakāh.

DATE:	✓	R

وَ ذٰلِكَ دِيْنُ الْقَيِّمَةِ ۵

And that is the correct religion.

اِنَّ الَّذِيْنَ كَفَرُوْا مِنْ اَهْلِ الْكِتٰبِ وَ الْمُشْرِكِيْنَ فِيْ نَارِ جَهَنَّمَ خٰلِدِيْنَ فِيْهَا

Surely those who disbelieved from among the People of the Book and the polytheists will be in the Fire of Hell, in which they will be living forever.

اُولٰٓئِكَ هُمْ شَرُّ الْبَرِيَّةِ ۶

Those are the worst of creatures.

اِنَّ الَّذِيْنَ اٰمَنُوْا وَ عَمِلُوا الصّٰلِحٰتِ اُولٰٓئِكَ هُمْ خَيْرُ الْبَرِيَّةِ ۷

Indeed, they who have believed and did righteous deeds - those are the best of creatures.

جَزَآؤُهُمْ عِنْدَ رَبِّهِمْ جَنّٰتُ عَدْنٍ تَجْرِيْ مِنْ تَحْتِهَا الْاَنْهٰرُ خٰلِدِيْنَ فِيْهَا اَبَدًا

Their reward with Allāh will be gardens of perpetual residence beneath which rivers flow, wherein they will abide forever,

رَضِيَ اللّٰهُ عَنْهُمْ وَ رَضُوْا عَنْهُ ذٰلِكَ لِمَنْ خَشِيَ رَبَّهُ ۸

Allāh being pleased with them and they with Him. That is for whoever has feared his Lord.

DATE: ✓ R

Sūrah Al-Qadr

بِسۡمِ اللّٰهِ الرَّحۡمٰنِ الرَّحِيۡمِ

In the name of Allāh, the Beneficent,
the Merciful.

اِنَّاۤ اَنۡزَلۡنٰهُ فِىۡ لَيۡلَةِ الۡقَدۡرِ ۚ ۖ ﴿۱﴾

Indeed, We sent the Qur'an down during the Night of Decree.

وَمَاۤ اَدۡرٰىكَ مَا لَيۡلَةُ الۡقَدۡرِ ؕ ﴿۲﴾

And what can make you know what is the Night of Decree?

لَيۡلَةُ الۡقَدۡرِ ۙ خَيۡرٌ مِّنۡ اَلۡفِ شَهۡرٍ ؕ ﴿۳﴾

The Night of Decree is better than a thousand months.

تَنَزَّلُ الۡمَلٰٓـئِكَةُ وَالرُّوۡحُ فِيۡهَا بِاِذۡنِ رَبِّهِمۡ‌ ۚ مِنۡ كُلِّ اَمۡرٍ ۛ ۙ ﴿۴﴾

The angels and the Spirit descend therein by permission
of their Lord for every matter.

سَلٰمٌ ۛ هِىَ حَتّٰى مَطۡلَعِ الۡفَجۡرِ ﴿۵﴾

Peace it is until the emergence of dawn.

DATE:	✓	R

Sūrah Al-'Alaq

بِسۡمِ اللّٰهِ الرَّحۡمٰنِ الرَّحِيۡمِ

In the name of Allāh, the Beneficent, the Merciful.

اِقۡرَاۡ بِاسۡمِ رَبِّكَ الَّذِىۡ خَلَقَ ۚ‏ ﴿۱﴾

Recite in the name of your Lord who created (everything),

خَلَقَ الۡاِنۡسَانَ مِنۡ عَلَقٍ ۚ‏ ﴿۲﴾

He created man from a clot of blood.

اِقۡرَاۡ وَرَبُّكَ الۡاَكۡرَمُ ۙ‏ ﴿۳﴾

Recite, and your Lord is the most Generous.

الَّذِىۡ عَلَّمَ بِالۡقَلَمِ ۙ‏ ﴿۴﴾

Who taught by the pen,

عَلَّمَ الۡاِنۡسَانَ مَا لَمۡ يَعۡلَمۡ ؕ‏ ﴿۵﴾

Taught man that which he did not know.

كَلَّاۤ اِنَّ الۡاِنۡسَانَ لَيَطۡغٰٓى ۙ‏ ﴿۶﴾

In fact, man crosses the limits,

اَنۡ رَّاٰهُ اسۡتَغۡنٰى ؕ‏ ﴿۷﴾

Because he sees himself self-sufficient.

DATE:	✓	R

Sūrah Al-'Alaq

إِنَّ إِلَىٰ رَبِّكَ الرُّجْعَىٰ ٨

Indeed, to your Lord is the return.

أَرَأَيْتَ الَّذِي يَنْهَىٰ ٩

Have you seen the one who forbids

عَبْدًا إِذَا صَلَّىٰ ١٠

A servant when he prays?

أَرَأَيْتَ إِن كَانَ عَلَى الْهُدَىٰ ١١

Have you seen if he is upon guidance

أَوْ أَمَرَ بِالتَّقْوَىٰ ١٢

Or enjoins righteousness?

أَرَأَيْتَ إِن كَذَّبَ وَتَوَلَّىٰ ١٣

Have you seen if he denies and turns away,

أَلَمْ يَعْلَم بِأَنَّ اللَّهَ يَرَىٰ ١٣

Does he not know that Allāh sees?

DATE:	✓	R

Sūrah Al-'Alaq

كَلَّا لَئِن لَّمْ يَنتَهِ لَنَسْفَعًا بِالنَّاصِيَةِ ﴿١٥﴾

No! If he does not desist, We will surely drag him by the forelock,

نَاصِيَةٍ كَاذِبَةٍ خَاطِئَةٍ ﴿١٦﴾

A lying, sinning forelock.

فَلْيَدْعُ نَادِيَهُ ﴿١٧﴾

Then let him call his associates;

سَنَدْعُ الزَّبَانِيَةَ ﴿١٨﴾

We will call the angels of Hell.

كَلَّا لَا تُطِعْهُ وَاسْجُدْ وَاقْتَرِب ﴿١٩﴾ السجدة

No! Do not obey him. But prostrate and draw near (to Allāh).

DATE: | ✓ | R

At-Ṭin

بِسْمِ اللّٰهِ الرَّحْمٰنِ الرَّحِيْمِ

In the name of Allāh, the Beneficent, the Merciful.

وَالتِّيْنِ وَالزَّيْتُوْنِ ﴿١﴾

(I take an oath) by the fig and the olive

وَطُوْرِ سِيْنِيْنَ ﴿٢﴾

And (by) Mount Sinai

وَهٰذَا الْبَلَدِ الْاَمِيْنِ ﴿٣﴾

And (by) this secure city (Makkah),

لَقَدْ خَلَقْنَا الْاِنْسَانَ فِيْٓ اَحْسَنِ تَقْوِيْمٍ ﴿٤﴾

We have created man in the best composition,

DATE:	✓	R

Sūrah At-Ṭin

ثُمَّ رَدَدْنٰهُ اَسْفَلَ سٰفِلِيْنَ ﴿٥﴾

Then We turned him into the lowest of the low,

اِلَّا الَّذِيْنَ اٰمَنُوْا وَعَمِلُوا الصّٰلِحٰتِ فَلَهُمْ اَجْرٌ غَيْرُ مَمْنُوْنٍ ﴿٦﴾

Except those who believed and did righteous deeds, because for them there is a never-ending reward.

فَمَا يُكَذِّبُكَ بَعْدُ بِالدِّيْنِ ﴿٧﴾

Then what (or who) causes you to deny the Day of Judgement?

اَلَيْسَ اللّٰهُ بِاَحْكَمِ الْحٰكِمِيْنَ ﴿٨﴾

Is not Allāh the best of judges?

DATE:	✓	R

C5 SŪRAH

Sūrah Al-Inshirāḥ

بِسۡمِ ٱللَّهِ ٱلرَّحۡمَٰنِ ٱلرَّحِيمِ

In the name of Allāh, the Beneficent, the Merciful.

أَلَمۡ نَشۡرَحۡ لَكَ صَدۡرَكَ ۝١ لا

Did We not expand for you, (O Muḥammad), your chest?

وَوَضَعۡنَا عَنكَ وِزۡرَكَ ۝٢ لا

And We removed from you your burden

ٱلَّذِيٓ أَنقَضَ ظَهۡرَكَ ۝٣ لا

Which had weighed upon your back

وَرَفَعۡنَا لَكَ ذِكۡرَكَ ۝۴ ط

And We raised high your name.

DATE: | ✓ | R

Sūrah Al-Inshiraḥ

فَإِنَّ مَعَ الْعُسْرِ يُسْرًا ۙ ﴿٥﴾

So, undoubtedly, along with the hardship there is ease.

إِنَّ مَعَ الْعُسْرِ يُسْرًا ؕ ﴿٦﴾

Undoubtedly, along with the hardship there is ease.

فَإِذَا فَرَغْتَ فَانْصَبْ ۙ ﴿٧﴾

So when you have finished (your duties), then stand up (for worship).

وَإِلَىٰ رَبِّكَ فَارْغَبْ ﴿٨﴾

And turn with eagerness towards your Lord.

DATE:	✓	R

Sūrah Adh-Duḥā

بِسۡمِ اللّٰهِ الرَّحۡمٰنِ الرَّحِيۡمِ

In the name of Allāh, the Beneficent, the Merciful.

وَالضُّحٰى ۙ﴿۱﴾

(I take an oath) by the morning brightness

وَالَّيۡلِ اِذَا سَجٰى ۙ﴿۲﴾

And (by) the night when it covers with darkness,

مَا وَدَّعَكَ رَبُّكَ وَمَا قَلٰى ؕ﴿۳﴾

Your Lord (O Prophet,) has neither forsaken you, nor has become displeased.

وَلَلۡاٰخِرَةُ خَيۡرٌ لَّكَ مِنَ الۡاُوۡلٰى ؕ﴿۴﴾

And the Hereafter is better for you than the first (life).

وَلَسَوۡفَ يُعۡطِيۡكَ رَبُّكَ فَتَرۡضٰى ؕ﴿۵﴾

And of course, your Lord will give you so much that you will be pleased.

DATE:	✓	R

Sūrah Adh-Duḥā

أَلَمْ يَجِدْكَ يَتِيمًا فَآوَىٰ ٦

Did He not find you an orphan, and give you shelter?

وَوَجَدَكَ ضَالًّا فَهَدَىٰ ٧

And He found you lost and guided (you),

وَوَجَدَكَ عَائِلًا فَأَغْنَىٰ ٨

And He found you poor and made (you) self-sufficient.

فَأَمَّا الْيَتِيمَ فَلَا تَقْهَرْ ٩

So as for the orphan, do not oppress (him).

وَأَمَّا السَّائِلَ فَلَا تَنْهَرْ ١٠

And as for the beggar, do not scold him.

وَأَمَّا بِنِعْمَةِ رَبِّكَ فَحَدِّثْ ١١

And about the bounty of your Lord, do talk.

DATE:	✓	R

Last 2 Āyāt of Sūrah Al-Baqarah

It was narrated from Abū Mas'ūd al-Anṣari رضي الله عنه that the Prophet صلى الله عليه وسلم said: "Whoever recites the last two verses of Sūrah Al-Baqarah at night, they will suffice him."

(Ṣaḥīḥ Bukhārī and Ṣaḥīḥ Muslim)

بِسْمِ اللَّهِ الرَّحْمَٰنِ الرَّحِيمِ

In the name of Allāh, the Beneficent, the Merciful.

آمَنَ الرَّسُولُ بِمَا أُنْزِلَ إِلَيْهِ مِنْ رَبِّهِ وَالْمُؤْمِنُونَ ۚ

The Messenger has believed in what has been revealed to him from his Lord, and the believers as well.

كُلٌّ آمَنَ بِاللَّهِ وَمَلَائِكَتِهِ وَكُتُبِهِ وَرُسُلِهِ لَا نُفَرِّقُ بَيْنَ أَحَدٍ مِنْ رُسُلِهِ

All have believed in Allāh and His angels and His books and His messengers. "We make no division between any of His messengers,"

وَقَالُوا سَمِعْنَا وَأَطَعْنَا ۖ غُفْرَانَكَ رَبَّنَا وَإِلَيْكَ الْمَصِيرُ ﴿٢٨٥﴾

...and they have said: "We have listened, and obeyed. Our Lord, (we seek) Your pardon! And to You is the return."

DATE:	✓	R

Last 2 Āyāt of Sūrah Al-Baqarah

لَا يُكَلِّفُ اللّٰهُ نَفْسًا اِلَّا وُسْعَهَا ؕ لَهَا مَا كَسَبَتْ وَعَلَيْهَا مَا اكْتَسَبَتْ ؕ

Allāh does not obligate anyone beyond his capacity. For him is what he has earned, and on him what he has incurred.

رَبَّنَا لَا تُؤَاخِذْنَآ اِنْ نَّسِيْنَآ اَوْ اَخْطَاْنَا ۚ

"Our Lord, do not hold us accountable, if we forget or make a mistake,

رَبَّنَا وَلَا تَحْمِلْ عَلَيْنَآ اِصْرًا كَمَا حَمَلْتَهٗ عَلَى الَّذِيْنَ مِنْ قَبْلِنَا

and, Our Lord, do not place on us such a burden as You have placed on those before us,

رَبَّنَا وَلَا تُحَمِّلْنَا مَا لَا طَاقَةَ لَنَا بِهٖ ۚ

and, Our Lord, do not make us bear a burden for which we have no strength.

وَاعْفُ عَنَّا ٚ وَاغْفِرْ لَنَا ٚ وَارْحَمْنَا ٚ اَنْتَ مَوْلٰىنَا فَانْصُرْنَا عَلَى الْقَوْمِ الْكٰفِرِيْنَ ۝٢٨٦ ع

And pardon us, and grant us forgiveness, and have mercy on us. You are our Lord. So then help us against the disbelieving people."

DATE:	✓	R

C6
SŪRAH

Sūrah Al-Kahf

Abud Dardā' رضي الله عنه reported Allāh's Messenger صلى الله عليه وسلم as saying: "If anyone learns by heart the first ten verses of the Sūrah Al-Kahf, he will be protected from the Dajjāl."

(Ṣaḥīḥ Muslim)

بِسْمِ اللهِ الرَّحْمٰنِ الرَّحِيْمِ

In the name of Allāh, the Beneficent,
the Merciful.

اَلْحَمْدُ لِلّٰهِ الَّذِيْٓ اَنْزَلَ عَلٰى عَبْدِهِ الْكِتٰبَ وَلَمْ يَجْعَلْ لَّهُ عِوَجًا ۜ ١

Praise belongs to Allāh who has sent down the Book to His servant, and allowed no crookedness in it,

قَيِّمًا لِّيُنْذِرَ بَأْسًا شَدِيْدًا مِّنْ لَّدُنْهُ وَيُبَشِّرَ الْمُؤْمِنِيْنَ الَّذِيْنَ يَعْمَلُوْنَ الصّٰلِحٰتِ

A straightforward Book to warn of a severe punishment from Him, and to give the good news to the believers, who do righteous deeds,

اَنَّ لَهُمْ اَجْرًا حَسَنًا ۙ ٢

that they will have an excellent reward (Paradise)

DATE: ☐ ✓ ☐ R

مَّاكِثِينَ فِيهِ أَبَدًا ۝٣

In which they will dwell for ever,

وَيُنذِرَ الَّذِينَ قَالُوا اتَّخَذَ اللَّهُ وَلَدًا ۝٤

And to warn those who have said that Allāh has had a son,

مَّا لَهُم بِهِ مِنْ عِلْمٍ وَلَا لِآبَائِهِمْ ۚ كَبُرَتْ كَلِمَةً تَخْرُجُ مِنْ أَفْوَاهِهِمْ ۚ إِن يَقُولُونَ إِلَّا كَذِبًا ۝٥

While they have no knowledge about it, nor had their fathers. Grave is the word that comes out of their mouths. They say nothing but lie.

فَلَعَلَّكَ بَاخِعٌ نَّفْسَكَ عَلَىٰ آثَارِهِمْ إِن لَّمْ يُؤْمِنُوا بِهَٰذَا الْحَدِيثِ أَسَفًا ۝٦

So, (O Prophet) perhaps you are going to kill yourself after them, out of grief, if they do not believe in this discourse.

إِنَّا جَعَلْنَا مَا عَلَى الْأَرْضِ زِينَةً لَّهَا لِنَبْلُوَهُمْ أَيُّهُمْ أَحْسَنُ عَمَلًا ۝٧

Surely, We have made what is on earth an adornment for it, so that We test them as to who among them is better in deeds.

DATE:	✓	R

وَإِنَّا لَجَٰعِلُونَ مَا عَلَيۡهَا صَعِيدٗا جُرُزًا ٨

And surely, We are going to turn whatever is thereon into a barren land.

أَمۡ حَسِبۡتَ أَنَّ أَصۡحَٰبَ ٱلۡكَهۡفِ وَٱلرَّقِيمِ كَانُواْ مِنۡ ءَايَٰتِنَا عَجَبًا ٩

Do you think that the People of Kahf (the Cave) and Raqīm (inscription) were unusual out of Our signs?

إِذۡ أَوَى ٱلۡفِتۡيَةُ إِلَى ٱلۡكَهۡفِ فَقَالُواْ رَبَّنَآ ءَاتِنَا مِن لَّدُنكَ رَحۡمَةٗ

When the young men took refuge in the Cave and said, "Our Lord, bless us with mercy from Your own...

وَهَيِّئۡ لَنَا مِنۡ أَمۡرِنَا رَشَدٗا

...and provide us with guidance in our matters."

DATE:	✓	R

Sūrah Al-Ḥashr

Ma'qil bin Yasār (رضي الله عنه) narrated that the Prophet (صلى الله عليه وسلم) said: "Whoever says three times when he gets up in the morning: 'A'ūdhu Billāhis-Samī' il-'Alīmi Minash-Shayṭānir-Rajīm' and he recites three Āyat from the end of Sūrah Al-Ḥashr - Allāh appoints seventy-thousand angels who say ṣalāt (mercy) upon him until the evening. If he dies on that day, he dies a martyr, and whoever reaches the evening, he holds the same status." (Tirmidhī)

بِسْمِ اللّٰهِ الرَّحْمٰنِ الرَّحِيْمِ

In the name of Allāh, the Beneficent, the Merciful.

هُوَ اللّٰهُ الَّذِىْ لَآ اِلٰهَ اِلَّا هُوَ ۚ عٰلِمُ الْغَيْبِ وَالشَّهَادَةِ ۚ هُوَ الرَّحْمٰنُ الرَّحِيْمُ ﴿٢٢﴾

He is Allāh, besides whom there is no God, the Knower of the unseen and the seen. He is All-Merciful, Very-Merciful.

هُوَ اللّٰهُ الَّذِىْ لَآ اِلٰهَ اِلَّا هُوَ ۚ اَلْمَلِكُ الْقُدُّوْسُ السَّلٰمُ الْمُؤْمِنُ الْمُهَيْمِنُ

He is Allāh, besides whom there is no God, the Sovereign, the Supreme-In-Holiness, the Safe (from all defects), the Giver-Of-Peace, the Guardian, the All-Mighty,

الْعَزِيْزُ الْجَبَّارُ الْمُتَكَبِّرُ ۗ سُبْحٰنَ اللّٰهِ عَمَّا يُشْرِكُوْنَ ﴿٢٣﴾

the All-Repairer, the Sublime. Pure is Allāh from what they associate with Him.

هُوَ اللّٰهُ الْخَالِقُ الْبَارِئُ الْمُصَوِّرُ لَهُ الْاَسْمَآءُ الْحُسْنٰى ۗ

He is Allāh, the Creator, the Inventor, the Shaper. His are the Most Beautiful Names.

يُسَبِّحُ لَهٗ مَا فِى السَّمٰوٰتِ وَالْاَرْضِ ۚ وَهُوَ الْعَزِيْزُ الْحَكِيْمُ ﴿٢٣﴾ ع

His purity is proclaimed by all that is in the heavens and the earth, and He is the All-Mighty, the All-Wise.

DATE:	✓	R

The Virtues of Sūrah Yāsīn

1. Anas ibn Mālik رضي الله عنه narrates that the Prophet صلى الله عليه وسلم said, "Everything has a heart and the heart of the Qur'ān is Yāsīn. So, whoever recites Yāsīn, Allāh will inscribe for him the reward of reciting the Qur'ān ten times." (Tirmidhī)

2. Abu Hurayrah رضي الله عنه narrates that the Prophet صلى الله عليه وسلم said, "Whoever recites Yāsīn at night, he will be forgiven." (Musnad, Abū Ya'alā) Some versions state, "Whoever recites Yāsīn in the morning and night..." (Tabarānī, Mu'ajam al-Saghīr)

3. Ibn Yasār رضي الله عنه narrates that the Prophet صلى الله عليه وسلم said, "Recite it on your dead." (Abū Dāwūd)

4. It is also narrated from some of the scholars that reciting Yāsīn eases one's hardships, as mentioned by Ibn Kathīr in his Tafsīr. There are also statements of the Prophet صلى الله عليه وسلم indicating so.

Sūrah Yāsīn

Our Beloved Prophet Muhammad صلى الله عليه وسلم said:

"Indeed in the Noble Qur'ān there is a sūrah, for its reading will intercede and will be a means of forgiveness for the listener. Listen carefully, it is Sūrah Yāsīn, in the Tawrah it is called Mu'immah."

It was enquired, "O' Messenger of Allāh, what is Muimmah?"

Our Beloved Prophet Muhammad صلى الله عليه وسلم replied:

"It contains for its reader the benefits of this world, it removes from him the dread of the next life, and it is called Dāfi'ah and Qāḍiyah."

It was asked again, "How is this sūrah Dāfi'ah and Qāḍiyah?"

Prophet صلى الله عليه وسلم replied:

"It takes away from its reader all afflictions and fulfils his need. Whoever recites it, it will be made equal to twenty pilgrimages. Whoever shall listen to it, it will be as a thousand dinars, which he has given as charity in the path of Allāh سبحانه وتعالى, and whoever shall write it and then drink it, it will enter into his heart a thousand cures, a thousand radiant lights, a thousand times more increase in belief, a thousand mercies, a thousand blessings, a thousand times more increase in guidance, and will remove from him all gall and disease." (Tirmidhī)

Sūrah Yāsīn

بِسۡمِ اللّٰهِ الرَّحۡمٰنِ الرَّحِيۡمِ

In the name of Allāh, the Beneficent, the Merciful.

يٰسٓ ﴿١﴾

Yāsīn

وَالۡقُرۡاٰنِ الۡحَكِيۡمِ ﴿٢﴾

By the Qur'ān, that is full of wisdom,

اِنَّكَ لَمِنَ الۡمُرۡسَلِيۡنَ ﴿٣﴾

You are truly one of the messengers of Allāh,

عَلٰى صِرَاطٍ مُّسۡتَقِيۡمٍ ﴿٤﴾

(and you are) on a straight path,

تَنۡزِيۡلَ الۡعَزِيۡزِ الرَّحِيۡمِ ﴿٥﴾

(this Qur'ān being) a revelation from the All- Mighty, the Very-Merciful,

لِتُنۡذِرَ قَوۡمًا مَّاۤ اُنۡذِرَ اٰبَآؤُهُمۡ فَهُمۡ غٰفِلُوۡنَ ﴿٦﴾

so that you may warn a people whose fathers were not warned, and hence, they are unaware.

لَقَدۡ حَقَّ الۡقَوۡلُ عَلٰٓى اَكۡثَرِهِمۡ فَهُمۡ لَا يُؤۡمِنُوۡنَ ﴿٧﴾

The word has indeed come true about most of them, so they will not believe.

DATE:	✓	R

Sūrah Yāsīn

إِنَّا جَعَلْنَا فِي أَعْنَاقِهِمْ أَغْلَالًا فَهِيَ إِلَى الْأَذْقَانِ فَهُمْ مُقْمَحُونَ ٨

We have placed iron collars on their necks, so they are reaching up to their chins, and their heads are forced to remain upwards.

وَجَعَلْنَا مِنْ بَيْنِ أَيْدِيهِمْ سَدًّا وَمِنْ خَلْفِهِمْ سَدًّا فَأَغْشَيْنَاهُمْ فَهُمْ لَا يُبْصِرُونَ ٩

And We have placed a barrier in front of them and a barrier behind them, and (thus) they are encircled by Us; so they do not see.

وَسَوَاءٌ عَلَيْهِمْ أَأَنْذَرْتَهُمْ أَمْ لَمْ تُنْذِرْهُمْ لَا يُؤْمِنُونَ ١٠

It is all equal for them whether you warn them or do not warn them, they will not believe.

إِنَّمَا تُنْذِرُ مَنِ اتَّبَعَ الذِّكْرَ وَخَشِيَ الرَّحْمَٰنَ بِالْغَيْبِ ۖ فَبَشِّرْهُ بِمَغْفِرَةٍ وَأَجْرٍ كَرِيمٍ ١١

You can (usefully) warn only the one who follows the advice and fears the Raḥmān (the All-Merciful Allāh) without seeing (Him). So give him the good news of forgiveness and of a noble reward.

إِنَّا نَحْنُ نُحْيِي الْمَوْتَىٰ وَنَكْتُبُ مَا قَدَّمُوا وَآثَارَهُمْ ۚ وَكُلَّ شَيْءٍ أَحْصَيْنَاهُ فِي إِمَامٍ مُبِينٍ ١٢

Surely We will give new life to the dead, and We are recording whatever (deeds) they send before them and whatever effects they leave behind. Everything is fully computed by Us in a manifest book of record.

وَاضْرِبْ لَهُمْ مَثَلًا أَصْحَابَ الْقَرْيَةِ إِذْ جَاءَهَا الْمُرْسَلُونَ ١٣

Cite to them the example of the people of the town, when the messengers came to it,

DATE:	✓	R

اِذۡ اَرۡسَلۡنَاۤ اِلَيۡهِمُ اثۡنَيۡنِ فَكَذَّبُوۡهُمَا فَعَزَّزۡنَا بِثَالِثٍ فَقَالُوۡۤا اِنَّاۤ اِلَيۡكُمۡ مُّرۡسَلُوۡنَ ۞

when We sent to them two (apostles), and they rejected both of them, so We confirmed them with a third one. So they said, "We are sent to you."

قَالُوۡا مَاۤ اَنۡتُمۡ اِلَّا بَشَرٌ مِّثۡلُنَا ۙ وَمَاۤ اَنۡزَلَ الرَّحۡمٰنُ مِنۡ شَيۡءٍ ۙ اِنۡ اَنۡتُمۡ اِلَّا تَكۡذِبُوۡنَ ۞

They (the people of the town) said, "You are no more than human beings like us, and the Raḥmān (the All-Merciful Allāh) has not sent down anything. You are but telling a lie."

قَالُوۡا رَبُّنَا يَعۡلَمُ اِنَّاۤ اِلَيۡكُمۡ لَمُرۡسَلُوۡنَ ۞

They (the messengers) said, "Our Lord knows that we are undoubtedly sent to you.

وَمَا عَلَيۡنَاۤ اِلَّا الۡبَلٰغُ الۡمُبِيۡنُ ۞

Our obligation is no more than to convey the message clearly."

قَالُوۡۤا اِنَّا تَطَيَّرۡنَا بِكُمۡ ۚ لَئِنۡ لَّمۡ تَنۡتَهُوۡا لَنَرۡجُمَنَّكُمۡ وَلَيَمَسَّنَّكُمۡ مِّنَّا عَذَابٌ اَلِيۡمٌ ۞

They (the people of the town) said, "We take you as a bad omen for us. If you do not desist, we will certainly stone you and you will be afflicted by a painful punishment from us."

قَالُوۡا طَاۤئِرُكُمۡ مَّعَكُمۡ ؕ اَئِنۡ ذُكِّرۡتُمۡ ؕ بَلۡ اَنۡتُمۡ قَوۡمٌ مُّسۡرِفُوۡنَ ۞

They said, "Your bad omen is with yourselves. (Do you take it as bad omen) if you are given a good counsel? Rather, you are a people who cross all limits."

DATE: ✓ R

Sūrah Yāsīn

وَجَآءَ مِنۡ اَقۡصَا الۡمَدِيۡنَةِ رَجُلٌ يَّسۡعٰى قَالَ يٰقَوۡمِ اتَّبِعُوا الۡمُرۡسَلِيۡنَ ۝٢٠

And there came a man rushing from the farthest part of the city. He said, "O my people, follow the messengers.

اتَّبِعُوۡا مَنۡ لَّا يَسۡـَٔلُكُمۡ اَجۡرًا وَّهُمۡ مُّهۡتَدُوۡنَ ۝٢١

Follow those who do not claim any reward from you, and who are on the right path.

وَمَا لِىَ لَاۤ اَعۡبُدُ الَّذِىۡ فَطَرَنِىۡ وَاِلَيۡهِ تُرۡجَعُوۡنَ ۝٢٢

What excuse do I have if I do not worship the One who has created me and to whom you will be returned?

ءَاَتَّخِذُ مِنۡ دُوۡنِهٖۤ اٰلِهَةً اِنۡ يُّرِدۡنِ الرَّحۡمٰنُ بِضُرٍّ لَّا تُغۡنِ عَنِّىۡ شَفَاعَتُهُمۡ شَيۡـًٔا وَّلَا يُنۡقِذُوۡنِ ۝٢٣

Shall I adopt those gods besides Him whose intercession, if Raḥmān (the All-Merciful Allāh) intends to do harm to me, cannot help me in the least, nor can they come to my rescue?

اِنِّىۡۤ اِذًا لَّفِىۡ ضَلٰلٍ مُّبِيۡنٍ ۝٢٤

In that case, I will be in open error indeed.

اِنِّىۡۤ اٰمَنۡتُ بِرَبِّكُمۡ فَاسۡمَعُوۡنِ ۝٢٥

Undoubtedly I have believed in your Lord; so listen to me."

DATE:	✓	R

Sūrah Yāsīn

قِيلَ ٱدْخُلِ ٱلْجَنَّةَ ۖ قَالَ يَٰلَيْتَ قَوْمِى يَعْلَمُونَ ﴿٢٦﴾

(Thereafter when his people killed him,) it was said to him, "Enter the Paradise". He said, "Would that my people knew

بِمَا غَفَرَ لِى رَبِّى وَجَعَلَنِى مِنَ ٱلْمُكْرَمِينَ ﴿٢٧﴾

how my Lord has forgiven me and placed me among the honoured ones!"

وَمَآ أَنزَلْنَا عَلَىٰ قَوْمِهِۦ مِنۢ بَعْدِهِۦ مِن جُندٍ مِّنَ ٱلسَّمَآءِ وَمَا كُنَّا مُنزِلِينَ ﴿٢٨﴾

And We did not send down to his people any army from the heavens after him, nor were We (in need) to send down.

إِن كَانَتْ إِلَّا صَيْحَةً وَٰحِدَةً فَإِذَا هُمْ خَٰمِدُونَ ﴿٢٩﴾

It was no more than a single cry, and in no time they were extinguished.

يَٰحَسْرَةً عَلَى ٱلْعِبَادِ ۚ مَا يَأْتِيهِم مِّن رَّسُولٍ إِلَّا كَانُوا۟ بِهِۦ يَسْتَهْزِءُونَ ﴿٣٠﴾

Alas for the slaves (of Allāh)! No messenger came to them, but they have been mocking him.

أَلَمْ يَرَوْا۟ كَمْ أَهْلَكْنَا قَبْلَهُم مِّنَ ٱلْقُرُونِ أَنَّهُمْ إِلَيْهِمْ لَا يَرْجِعُونَ ﴿٣١﴾

Did they not see how many generations We have destroyed before them who will not come back to them?

DATE:	✓	R

وَاِنْ كُلٌّ لَّمَّا جَمِيعٌ لَّدَيْنَا مُحْضَرُوْنَ ۝

All of them are but to be assembled together (and) to be arraigned before Us.

وَاٰيَةٌ لَّهُمُ الْاَرْضُ الْمَيْتَةُ ۚ اَحْيَيْنٰهَا وَاَخْرَجْنَا مِنْهَا حَبًّا فَمِنْهُ يَاْكُلُوْنَ ۝

And a sign for them is the dead land. We gave it life and brought forth grain from it; so from it they eat.

وَجَعَلْنَا فِيْهَا جَنّٰتٍ مِّنْ نَّخِيْلٍ وَّاَعْنَابٍ وَّفَجَّرْنَا فِيْهَا مِنَ الْعُيُوْنِ ۝

And We have placed gardens of date-palms and grapes, and caused springs to gush forth therein,

لِيَاْكُلُوْا مِنْ ثَمَرِهٖ ۙ وَمَا عَمِلَتْهُ اَيْدِيْهِمْ ؕ اَفَلَا يَشْكُرُوْنَ ۝

so that they may eat fruits thereof, while it was not made by their hands. Would they not then offer gratitude?

سُبْحٰنَ الَّذِيْ خَلَقَ الْاَزْوَاجَ كُلَّهَا مِمَّا تُنْۢبِتُ الْاَرْضُ وَمِنْ اَنْفُسِهِمْ وَمِمَّا لَا يَعْلَمُوْنَ ۝

Pure (from every fault) is the One who has created all the pairs of whatever the earth grows and of the humans themselves and of that which they do not know.

وَاٰيَةٌ لَّهُمُ الَّيْلُ ۖ نَسْلَخُ مِنْهُ النَّهَارَ فَاِذَا هُمْ مُّظْلِمُوْنَ ۝

And a sign for them is the night. We strip (the cover of) the day from it, and they are suddenly in darkness.

DATE:	✓	R

Sūrah Yāsīn

وَالشَّمْسُ تَجْرِيْ لِمُسْتَقَرٍّ لَّهَا ۚ ذٰلِكَ تَقْدِيْرُ الْعَزِيْزِ الْعَلِيْمِ ۝

And the sun is quickly proceeding towards its destination. That is the designing of the All-Mighty, the All-Knowing.

وَالْقَمَرَ قَدَّرْنٰهُ مَنَازِلَ حَتّٰى عَادَ كَالْعُرْجُوْنِ الْقَدِيْمِ ۝

And for the moon We have appointed measured phases, until it turned (pale, curved and fine) like an old branch of date palm.

لَا الشَّمْسُ يَنْۢبَغِيْ لَهَآ اَنْ تُدْرِكَ الْقَمَرَ وَلَا الَّيْلُ سَابِقُ النَّهَارِ ۚ وَكُلٌّ فِيْ فَلَكٍ يَّسْبَحُوْنَ ۝

Neither it is for the sun to overtake the moon, nor can the night outpace the day. Each one is floating in an orbit.

وَاٰيَةٌ لَّهُمْ اَنَّا حَمَلْنَا ذُرِّيَّتَهُمْ فِى الْفُلْكِ الْمَشْحُوْنِ ۝

And it is a sign for them that We boarded their children in the loaded ship,

وَخَلَقْنَا لَهُمْ مِّنْ مِّثْلِهٖ مَا يَرْكَبُوْنَ ۝

and created for them things similar to it on which they ride.

وَاِنْ نَّشَاْ نُغْرِقْهُمْ فَلَا صَرِيْخَ لَهُمْ وَلَا هُمْ يُنْقَذُوْنَ ۝

And if We so will, We can drown them; then no one will respond to their cry, nor will they be rescued,

اِلَّا رَحْمَةً مِّنَّا وَمَتَاعًا اِلٰى حِيْنٍ ۝

unless there be mercy from Us, and (unless) We let them enjoy for a while.

وَاِذَا قِيْلَ لَهُمُ اتَّقُوْا مَا بَيْنَ اَيْدِيْكُمْ وَمَا خَلْفَكُمْ لَعَلَّكُمْ تُرْحَمُوْنَ ۝

And (they pay no heed) when it is said to them, "Save yourselves from that (punishment) which is before you (in this world) and that which will come after you (die), so that you may receive mercy".

DATE: ☐ ✓ R

وَمَا تَأْتِيهِم مِّنْ اٰيَةٍ مِّنْ اٰيٰتِ رَبِّهِمْ إِلَّا كَانُوْا عَنْهَا مُعْرِضِيْنَ ۝

There comes to them no sign from the signs of your Lord, but they turn averse to it.

وَإِذَا قِيْلَ لَهُمْ أَنْفِقُوْا مِمَّا رَزَقَكُمُ اللّٰهُ ۙ قَالَ الَّذِيْنَ كَفَرُوْا لِلَّذِيْنَ اٰمَنُوْا أَنُطْعِمُ مَنْ لَّوْ يَشَآءُ ۝

And when it is said to them, "Spend (to the needy) from the provision Allāh has given to you", the disbelievers say to the believers,

اللّٰهُ أَطْعَمَهٗ ۖ إِنْ أَنْتُمْ إِلَّا فِيْ ضَلٰلٍ مُّبِيْنٍ ۝

"Shall we feed those whom Allāh could have fed, if Allāh so willed? You are but in open error."

وَيَقُوْلُوْنَ مَتٰى هٰذَا الْوَعْدُ إِنْ كُنْتُمْ صٰدِقِيْنَ ۝

And they say, "When will this promise come true, if you are truthful?"

مَا يَنْظُرُوْنَ إِلَّا صَيْحَةً وَّاحِدَةً تَأْخُذُهُمْ وَهُمْ يَخِصِّمُوْنَ ۝

They are looking for nothing but for a single cry that will seize them when they will be quarrelling.

فَلَا يَسْتَطِيْعُوْنَ تَوْصِيَةً وَّلَآ إِلٰى أَهْلِهِمْ يَرْجِعُوْنَ ۝

So they will not be able to make a bequest, nor will they return to their household.

DATE: ✓ R

C7
SŪRAH

Sūrah Yāsīn

بِسْمِ اللهِ الرَّحْمٰنِ الرَّحِيْمِ

In the name of Allāh, the Beneficent,
the Merciful.

وَنُفِخَ فِى الصُّوْرِ فَاِذَا هُمْ مِّنَ الْاَجْدَاثِ اِلٰى رَبِّهِمْ يَنْسِلُوْنَ ۝

And the Horn will be blown, and suddenly they will be rushing
from their graves towards their Lord.

قَالُوْا يٰوَيْلَنَا مَنْۢ بَعَثَنَا مِنْ مَّرْقَدِنَا ۜ هٰذَا مَا وَعَدَ الرَّحْمٰنُ وَصَدَقَ الْمُرْسَلُوْنَ ۝

They will say, "Woe to us! Who has raised us from our sleeping
place? "This is what Raḥmān (the All-Merciful Allāh) had
promised, and the messengers had told the truth.

اِنْ كَانَتْ اِلَّا صَيْحَةً وَّاحِدَةً فَاِذَا هُمْ جَمِيْعٌ لَّدَيْنَا مُحْضَرُوْنَ ۝

It will be no more than a single Cry, and in no time they will all
be arraigned before Us.

فَالْيَوْمَ لَا تُظْلَمُ نَفْسٌ شَيْئًا وَّلَا تُجْزَوْنَ اِلَّا مَا كُنْتُمْ تَعْمَلُوْنَ ۝

Then, nobody will be subjected to injustice in the least, and
you will not be recompensed but for what you used to do.

DATE: √ R

Sūrah Yāsīn

إِنَّ أَصْحَٰبَ ٱلْجَنَّةِ ٱلْيَوْمَ فِى شُغُلٍ فَٰكِهُونَ ٥٥

The people of the Paradise are engaged today in (their) activities, happily enjoying (them).

هُمْ وَأَزْوَٰجُهُمْ فِى ظِلَٰلٍ عَلَى ٱلْأَرَآئِكِ مُتَّكِـُٔونَ ٥٦

They and their spouses are in pleasant shades, reclining on couches.

لَهُمْ فِيهَا فَٰكِهَةٌ وَلَهُم مَّا يَدَّعُونَ ٥٧

For them there are fruits, and for them there is whatever they ask for.

سَلَٰمٌ قَوْلًا مِّن رَّبٍّ رَّحِيمٍ ٥٨

"Salām "(Peace upon you) is the word (they receive) from the Merciful Lord.

وَٱمْتَٰزُوا۟ ٱلْيَوْمَ أَيُّهَا ٱلْمُجْرِمُونَ ٥٩

And (it will be said to the infidels,) "Get apart (from the believers) today, O the guilty ones.

أَلَمْ أَعْهَدْ إِلَيْكُمْ يَٰبَنِىٓ ءَادَمَ أَن لَّا تَعْبُدُوا۟ ٱلشَّيْطَٰنَ ۖ إِنَّهُۥ لَكُمْ عَدُوٌّ مُّبِينٌ ٦٠

Did I not direct you, O children of 'Ādam (Adam), that you must not worship the Satan, (because) he is an open enemy for you,

DATE:	✓	R

Sūrah Yāsīn

وَّاَنِ اعْبُدُوْنِیْ ؕ هٰذَا صِرَاطٌ مُّسْتَقِیْمٌ ﴿٦١﴾

and that you must worship Me, (because) this is the straight path.

وَلَقَدْ اَضَلَّ مِنْكُمْ جِبِلًّا كَثِیْرًا ؕ اَفَلَمْ تَكُوْنُوْا تَعْقِلُوْنَ ﴿٦٢﴾

He had misguided many people from among you. So, did you not have sense?

هٰذِهٖ جَهَنَّمُ الَّتِیْ كُنْتُمْ تُوْعَدُوْنَ ﴿٦٣﴾

(Now) this is the Jahannam of which you were consistently warned.

اِصْلَوْهَا الْیَوْمَ بِمَا كُنْتُمْ تَكْفُرُوْنَ ﴿٦٤﴾

Enter it today, because you have been persistently denying (the truth)."

اَلْیَوْمَ نَخْتِمُ عَلٰۤی اَفْوَاهِهِمْ وَتُكَلِّمُنَاۤ اَیْدِیْهِمْ وَتَشْهَدُ اَرْجُلُهُمْ بِمَا كَانُوْا یَكْسِبُوْنَ ﴿٦٥﴾

Today We will set a seal on their mouths, and their hands will speak to Us, and their legs will bear witness about what they used to do.

وَلَوْ نَشَآءُ لَطَمَسْنَا عَلٰۤی اَعْیُنِهِمْ فَاسْتَبَقُوا الصِّرَاطَ فَاَنّٰی یُبْصِرُوْنَ ﴿٦٦﴾

If We so will, We would wipe out their eyes (right here in this world), and they would be racing towards the way, but how would they see?

DATE:	✓	R

Sūrah Yāsīn

وَلَوْ نَشَآءُ لَمَسَخْنٰهُمْ عَلٰى مَكَانَتِهِمْ فَمَا اسْتَطَاعُوْا مُضِيًّا وَّلَا يَرْجِعُوْنَ ﴿٦٧﴾

And If We did so will, We would disfigure them at their places, and they would not be able to move, nor would they return.

وَمَنْ نُّعَمِّرْهُ نُنَكِّسْهُ فِى الْخَلْقِ ؕ اَفَلَا يَعْقِلُوْنَ ﴿٦٨﴾

And whomsoever We give long life, we reverse him in creation. Then, do they have no sense?

وَمَا عَلَّمْنٰهُ الشِّعْرَ وَمَا يَنْۢبَغِىْ لَهٗ ؕ اِنْ هُوَ اِلَّا ذِكْرٌ وَّقُرْاٰنٌ مُّبِيْنٌ ﴿٦٩﴾

We did not teach him (the Holy Prophet) poetry, and it is not proper for him. It is nothing (of that sort,) but (it is) an advice and a readable book that explains (the Truth),

لِّيُنْذِرَ مَنْ كَانَ حَيًّا وَّيَحِقَّ الْقَوْلُ عَلَى الْكٰفِرِيْنَ ﴿٧٠﴾

so that it may warn him who is alive (to listen to the truth), and so that the word may prove true against the disbelievers.

اَوَلَمْ يَرَوْا اَنَّا خَلَقْنَا لَهُمْ مِّمَّا عَمِلَتْ اَيْدِيْنَاۤ اَنْعَامًا فَهُمْ لَهَا مٰلِكُوْنَ ﴿٧١﴾

Did they not see that We have created for them cattle, among things made (directly) by Our hands, and then they become their owners?

وَذَلَّلْنٰهَا لَهُمْ فَمِنْهَا رَكُوْبُهُمْ وَمِنْهَا يَاْكُلُوْنَ ﴿٧٢﴾

And We have brought them under their control, so as some of them are their means of transport, and some of them they eat.

DATE:	✓	R

Sūrah Yāsīn

وَلَهُمْ فِيهَا مَنَافِعُ وَمَشَارِبُ ۖ أَفَلَا يَشْكُرُونَ ﴿٧٣﴾

And for them there are (other) benefits in them and things to drink. So, would they not be grateful?

وَاتَّخَذُوا مِنْ دُونِ اللَّهِ آلِهَةً لَعَلَّهُمْ يُنْصَرُونَ ﴿٧٤﴾

They have adopted gods other than Allāh, so that they may be helped (by them).

لَا يَسْتَطِيعُونَ نَصْرَهُمْ ۙ وَهُمْ لَهُمْ جُنْدٌ مُحْضَرُونَ ﴿٧٥﴾

They cannot help them, rather they (the disbelievers themselves) are (like) an army brought forth for (protecting) them (the so-called co-gods)

فَلَا يَحْزُنْكَ قَوْلُهُمْ ۘ إِنَّا نَعْلَمُ مَا يُسِرُّونَ وَمَا يُعْلِنُونَ ﴿٧٦﴾

So, their remarks must not grieve you. Surely We know what they conceal and what they disclose.

أَوَلَمْ يَرَ الْإِنْسَانُ أَنَّا خَلَقْنَاهُ مِنْ نُطْفَةٍ فَإِذَا هُوَ خَصِيمٌ مُبِينٌ ﴿٧٧﴾

Did man not see that We have created him from a drop of semen? Then suddenly he stood as an open adversary (to Us).

وَضَرَبَ لَنَا مَثَلًا وَنَسِيَ خَلْقَهُ ۖ قَالَ مَنْ يُحْيِي الْعِظَامَ وَهِيَ رَمِيمٌ ﴿٧٨﴾

He has set up an argument about Us and forgot his creation. He said, "Who will give life to the bones when they are decayed?"

DATE:	✓	R

Sūrah Yāsīn

قُلْ يُحْيِيهَا الَّذِيٓ أَنْشَأَهَآ أَوَّلَ مَرَّةٍ ۖ وَهُوَ بِكُلِّ خَلْقٍ عَلِيمٌ ﴿٧٩﴾

Say, "These will be revived by the same One who had created them for the first time, and who is fully aware of every creation,

الَّذِي جَعَلَ لَكُمْ مِّنَ الشَّجَرِ الْأَخْضَرِ نَارًا فَإِذَآ أَنْتُمْ مِّنْهُ تُوقِدُونَ ﴿٨٠﴾

- the One who created for you fire from the green tree, and in no time you kindle from it."

أَوَلَيْسَ الَّذِي خَلَقَ السَّمٰوٰتِ وَالْأَرْضَ بِقٰدِرٍ عَلٰٓى أَنْ يَّخْلُقَ مِثْلَهُمْ ۚ بَلٰى ۗ وَهُوَ الْخَلّٰقُ الْعَلِيمُ ﴿٨١﴾

Is it that the One who has created the heavens and the earth has no power to create ones like them? Why not? He is the Supreme Creator, the All-Knowing.

إِنَّمَآ أَمْرُهٗٓ إِذَآ أَرَادَ شَيْـًٔا أَنْ يَّقُولَ لَهٗ كُنْ فَيَكُونُ ﴿٨٢﴾

His practice, when He intends to do something, is no more than He says, "Be", and it comes to be.

فَسُبْحٰنَ الَّذِي بِيَدِهٖ مَلَكُوتُ كُلِّ شَيْءٍ وَّإِلَيْهِ تُرْجَعُونَ ﴿٨٣﴾

So, pure (from every fault) is the One in whose hand is the dominion of all things. And towards Him you are to be returned.

DATE:	✓	R

Sūrah As-Sajdah

The Virtues of Sūrah As-Sajdah

1. Sayyidina Jābir رضي الله عنه narrates that the Holy Prophet صلى الله عليه وسلم would not retire to bed until he had recited Alif Lām Tanzīl and Tabārakalaẓi biyadihil mulk. (Tirmiḍi)

2. Sayyidina Khalid ibn Ma'dan رضي الله عنه said, "Recite the Deliverer, which is Alif Lām Tanzīl, for I have heard that a man who had committed many sins used to recite it and nothing else. It spread its wing over him and said, 'O' My Lord, forgive him, for he often used to recite me.' So the Lord Most High made it an intercessor for him and said, 'Record for him a good deed and raise him a degree in place of every sin."

Sūrah As-Sajdah

Sayyidina Khalid رضي الله عنه also said, "It will dispute on behalf of the one who recites it when he is in his grave saying, 'O' Allāh, if I am part of your Book, make me an intercessor for him. But if I am not a part of your Book, remove me out of it.' It will be like a bird putting its wing on him, it will intercede for him and will protect him from the punishment in the grave." He said the same about Tabārakallaẓi (Sūrah Mulk). Sayyidina Khalid رضي الله عنه did not go to sleep at night till he had recited them. Ṭāūs said that they were given sixty virtues more than any other sūrah in the Holy Qur'ān. (Dāramī)

Sūrah As-Sajdah

بِسۡمِ اللّٰہِ الرَّحۡمٰنِ الرَّحِیۡمِ

In the name of Allāh, the Beneficent,
the Merciful.

الٓـمّٓ ۚ﴿۱﴾

Alif. Lam. Mim

تَنۡزِیۡلُ الۡکِتٰبِ لَا رَیۡبَ فِیۡہِ مِنۡ رَّبِّ الۡعٰلَمِیۡنَ ؕ﴿۲﴾

(This) revelation of the Book - in which there is no doubt - is from the Lord of the worlds.

اَمۡ یَقُوۡلُوۡنَ افۡتَرٰىہُ ۚ بَلۡ ہُوَ الۡحَقُّ مِنۡ رَّبِّکَ لِتُنۡذِرَ قَوۡمًا مَّاۤ اَتٰىہُمۡ مِّنۡ نَّذِیۡرٍ مِّنۡ قَبۡلِکَ لَعَلَّہُمۡ یَہۡتَدُوۡنَ ﴿۳﴾

Is it that they say, "He has fabricated it."? No, it is the truth from your Lord, so that you (O Prophet) may warn a people to whom no warner has come before you; maybe they take the right path.

اَللّٰہُ الَّذِیۡ خَلَقَ السَّمٰوٰتِ وَ الۡاَرۡضَ وَ مَا بَیۡنَہُمَا فِیۡ سِتَّۃِ اَیَّامٍ ثُمَّ اسۡتَوٰی عَلَی الۡعَرۡشِ ؕ

مَا لَکُمۡ مِّنۡ دُوۡنِہٖ مِنۡ وَّلِیٍّ وَّ لَا شَفِیۡعٍ ؕ اَفَلَا تَتَذَکَّرُوۡنَ ﴿۴﴾

Allāh is the One who created the heavens and the earth and all that is between them in six days, then He positioned Himself on the Throne. Other than Him, there is neither a guardian for you, nor an intercessor. Would you then not observe the advice?

DATE:	✓	R

Sūrah As-Sajdah

يُدَبِّرُ ٱلْأَمْرَ مِنَ ٱلسَّمَآءِ إِلَى ٱلْأَرْضِ ثُمَّ يَعْرُجُ إِلَيْهِ فِى يَوْمٍ كَانَ مِقْدَارُهُۥٓ أَلْفَ سَنَةٍ مِّمَّا تَعُدُّونَ ﴿٥﴾

He manages (every) matter from the sky to the earth, then it (every matter) will ascend to Him in a day the measure of which is one thousand years according to the way you count.

ذَٰلِكَ عَٰلِمُ ٱلْغَيْبِ وَٱلشَّهَٰدَةِ ٱلْعَزِيزُ ٱلرَّحِيمُ ﴿٦﴾

That One is the All-Knower of the unseen and the seen, the All-Mighty, the Very-Merciful,

ٱلَّذِىٓ أَحْسَنَ كُلَّ شَىْءٍ خَلَقَهُۥ ۖ وَبَدَأَ خَلْقَ ٱلْإِنسَٰنِ مِن طِينٍ ﴿٧﴾

Who made all things good which He created, and He began the creation of man from clay;

ثُمَّ جَعَلَ نَسْلَهُۥ مِن سُلَٰلَةٍ مِّن مَّآءٍ مَّهِينٍ ﴿٨﴾

Then He made his progeny from a drop of semen, from despised water.

ثُمَّ سَوَّىٰهُ وَنَفَخَ فِيهِ مِن رُّوحِهِۦ ۖ وَجَعَلَ لَكُمُ ٱلسَّمْعَ وَٱلْأَبْصَٰرَ وَٱلْأَفْـِٔدَةَ ۚ قَلِيلًا مَّا تَشْكُرُونَ ﴿٩﴾

Then He gave him a proportioned shape, and breathed into him of His spirit. And He granted you the (power of) hearing and the eyes and the hearts. Little do you give thanks.

وَقَالُوٓا۟ أَءِذَا ضَلَلْنَا فِى ٱلْأَرْضِ أَءِنَّا لَفِى خَلْقٍ جَدِيدٍۭ ۚ بَلْ هُم بِلِقَآءِ رَبِّهِمْ كَٰفِرُونَ ﴿١٠﴾

And they said, "Is it that when we disappear in the earth, will we really come into a new creation?" Rather they are ones who deny the meeting with their Lord.

DATE:	✓	R

Sūrah As-Sajdah

قُلْ يَتَوَفّٰىكُمْ مَّلَكُ الْمَوْتِ الَّذِىْ وُكِّلَ بِكُمْ ثُمَّ اِلٰى رَبِّكُمْ تُرْجَعُوْنَ ﴿١١﴾

Say, "The angel of death who has been assigned for you will take your soul in full, then you will be brought back to your Lord."

وَلَوْ تَرٰٓى اِذِ الْمُجْرِمُوْنَ نَاكِسُوْا رُءُوْسِهِمْ عِنْدَ رَبِّهِمْ

رَبَّنَآ اَبْصَرْنَا وَسَمِعْنَا فَارْجِعْنَا نَعْمَلْ صَالِحًا اِنَّا مُوْقِنُوْنَ ﴿١٢﴾

And (you will wonder) if you see the sinners hanging their heads before their Lord (and saying,) "Our Lord, we have now seen and heard, so send us back, and we will do righteous deeds. Surely, (now) we are believers."

وَلَوْ شِئْنَا لَاٰتَيْنَا كُلَّ نَفْسٍ هُدٰىهَا وَلٰكِنْ حَقَّ الْقَوْلُ مِنِّىْ لَاَمْلَئَنَّ جَهَنَّمَ مِنَ الْجِنَّةِ وَالنَّاسِ اَجْمَعِيْنَ ﴿١٣﴾

And if We had so willed, We would have led everybody to his right path (by force), but the word from Me had come to pass: "I will certainly fill the Jahannam with jinn and human beings together."

فَذُوْقُوْا بِمَا نَسِيْتُمْ لِقَآءَ يَوْمِكُمْ هٰذَا ۚ اِنَّا نَسِيْنٰكُمْ وَذُوْقُوْا عَذَابَ الْخُلْدِ بِمَا كُنْتُمْ تَعْمَلُوْنَ ﴿١٣﴾

So, have a taste, because you had forgotten the meeting of this day of yours. We have forgotten you; and taste the eternal punishment for what you used to do.

اِنَّمَا يُؤْمِنُ بِاٰيٰتِنَا الَّذِيْنَ اِذَا ذُكِّرُوْا بِهَا خَرُّوْا سُجَّدًا وَّسَبَّحُوْا بِحَمْدِ رَبِّهِمْ وَهُمْ لَا يَسْتَكْبِرُوْنَ ﴿١٥﴾ السجدة

Only those people believe in Our verses who, when they are reminded of them, fall in prostration and pronounce the purity and praise of their Lord, and who are not proud.

DATE:	✓	R

تَتَجَافٰى جُنُوبُهُمْ عَنِ الْمَضَاجِعِ يَدْعُوْنَ رَبَّهُمْ خَوْفًا وَّطَمَعًا ۖ وَّمِمَّا رَزَقْنٰهُمْ يُنْفِقُوْنَ ۞

Their sides remain apart from their beds. They call their Lord with fear and hope, and spend (in charity) out of what We have given to them.

فَلَا تَعْلَمُ نَفْسٌ مَّآ أُخْفِيَ لَهُمْ مِّنْ قُرَّةِ أَعْيُنٍ ۚ جَزَآءً ۢ بِمَا كَانُوْا يَعْمَلُوْنَ ۞

So, no one knows the delight of the eyes that has been reserved for them in secret, as a reward of what they used to do.

أَفَمَنْ كَانَ مُؤْمِنًا كَمَنْ كَانَ فَاسِقًا ۚ لَا يَسْتَوٗنَ ۞

So, can one who is a believer become like one who is a sinner? They cannot become equal.

أَمَّا الَّذِيْنَ اٰمَنُوْا وَعَمِلُوا الصّٰلِحٰتِ فَلَهُمْ جَنّٰتُ الْمَأْوٰى ۖ نُزُلًا ۢ بِمَا كَانُوْا يَعْمَلُوْنَ ۞

As for those who believe and do righteous deeds, for them there are gardens in which to dwell, as an honorable hospitality for what they used to do.

وَأَمَّا الَّذِيْنَ فَسَقُوْا فَمَأْوٰىهُمُ النَّارُ ۖ كُلَّمَآ أَرَادُوٓا أَنْ يَّخْرُجُوْا مِنْهَآ أُعِيْدُوْا فِيْهَا وَقِيْلَ لَهُمْ

ذُوْقُوْا عَذَابَ النَّارِ الَّذِيْ كُنْتُمْ بِهٖ تُكَذِّبُوْنَ ۞

And the ones who disobeyed, their abode is the Fire. Whenever they wish to come out from it, they will be turned back into it, and it will be said to them, "Taste the punishment of fire that you used to deny."

DATE: ✓ R

Sūrah As-Sajdah

وَلَنُذِيقَنَّهُمْ مِّنَ الْعَذَابِ الْأَدْنَى دُونَ الْعَذَابِ الْأَكْبَرِ لَعَلَّهُمْ يَرْجِعُوْنَ ۝

And We will certainly make them taste the nearer punishment before the greater punishment, so that they may return.

وَمَنْ أَظْلَمُ مِمَّنْ ذُكِّرَ بِأَيَتِ رَبِّهِ ثُمَّ أَعْرَضَ عَنْهَا ۚ إِنَّا مِنَ الْمُجْرِمِيْنَ مُنْتَقِمُوْنَ ۝

And who is more unjust than the one who was reminded of the verses of his Lord, then he turned away from them. Surely, We have to take vengeance upon the sinners.

وَلَقَدْ اٰتَيْنَا مُوْسَى الْكِتٰبَ فَلَا تَكُنْ فِيْ مِرْيَةٍ مِّنْ لِّقَآئِهٖ وَجَعَلْنٰهُ هُدًى لِّبَنِيْ اِسْرَآءِيْلَ ۝

It is a fact that We gave the Book to Mūsā. So be not in doubt about receiving it, and We made it a guidance for the children of Isrā'īl .

وَجَعَلْنَا مِنْهُمْ أَئِمَّةً يَّهْدُوْنَ بِأَمْرِنَا لَمَّا صَبَرُوْا ۖ وَكَانُوْا بِأَيٰتِنَا يُوْقِنُوْنَ ۝

And We appointed leaders from among them who guided (people) under Our command, when they observed patience, and kept firm belief in Our verses.

إِنَّ رَبَّكَ هُوَ يَفْصِلُ بَيْنَهُمْ يَوْمَ الْقِيٰمَةِ فِيْمَا كَانُوْا فِيْهِ يَخْتَلِفُوْنَ ۝

Surely, your Lord will judge between them on the Day of Judgement in what they used to differ.

DATE: ✓ R

Sūrah As-Sajdah

أَوَلَمْ يَهْدِ لَهُمْ كَمْ أَهْلَكْنَا مِن قَبْلِهِم مِّنَ الْقُرُونِ يَمْشُونَ فِي مَسَاكِنِهِمْ ط

إِنَّ فِي ذَٰلِكَ لَآيَاتٍ ط أَفَلَا يَسْمَعُونَ ﴿٢٦﴾

Has it not been a source of guidance for them as to how many generations We have destroyed before them who used to walk in their dwellings? Surely in this there are signs. So, do they not listen?

أَوَلَمْ يَرَوْا أَنَّا نَسُوقُ الْمَاءَ إِلَى الْأَرْضِ الْجُرُزِ فَنُخْرِجُ بِهِ زَرْعًا تَأْكُلُ مِنْهُ أَنْعَامُهُمْ وَأَنفُسُهُمْ ط

أَفَلَا يُبْصِرُونَ ﴿٢٧﴾ الثلثة

Have they not seen that We drive water to the dry land, then We bring forth crops thereby from which their cattle and they themselves have food? So, do they not see?

وَيَقُولُونَ مَتَىٰ هَٰذَا الْفَتْحُ إِن كُنتُمْ صَادِقِينَ ﴿٢٨﴾

And they say, "When will this decision take place if you are truthful (in your claim)?"

قُلْ يَوْمَ الْفَتْحِ لَا يَنفَعُ الَّذِينَ كَفَرُوا إِيمَانُهُمْ وَلَا هُمْ يُنظَرُونَ ﴿٢٩﴾

Say, "On the day of decision their belief will not be of any use to disbelievers, nor shall they be given any respite."

فَأَعْرِضْ عَنْهُمْ وَانتَظِرْ إِنَّهُم مُّنتَظِرُونَ ﴿٣٠﴾ ع

So, just ignore them (O prophet,) and wait. They (too) are waiting.

DATE:	✓	R

C8
SŪRAH

Sūrah Al-Mulk

The Virtues of Sūrah Al-Mulk

1. Sayyidina Abū Hurayrah رضي الله عنه reported Allāh Ta'ālā's Messenger صلى الله عليه وسلم as saying, "A sūrah in the Qur'ān containing thirty verses interceded for a man untill his sins were forgiven. It was Tabārakalladhī Biyadihil Mulk."
(Tirmidhī, (Abū Dāwūd), Nasai and Ibn Majah)

2. Sayyidina Ibn Abbās رضي الله عنه said that one of the Prophet's صلى الله عليه وسلم Companions set up his tent over a grave without realising that it was a grave and it contained a man who was reciting the Sūrah Tabārakalladhi Biyadihil Mulk up to the end. He went and told the Holy Prophet صلى الله عليه وسلم who said, "It is The Defender; it is The Protector which safeguards one from Allāh's punishment."
(Tirmidhī)

3. Sayyidina Jabir رضي الله عنه said it was the custom of the Holy Prophet صلى الله عليه وسلم not to go to sleep until he had read Tabārakalladhi Biyadihil Mulk and Alif Lām Mīm Tanzīl.
(Aḥmad, Tirmidhī and Dāramī)

4. Sayyidina Anas رضي الله عنه reported Rasūlullāh صلى الله عليه وسلم as saying, "There is a sūrah which will plead for its reciter till it causes him to enter Paradise (Tabārakalladhī Biyadihil Mulk)." (Ṭabarānī)

5. Sayyidina Ibn Abbās رضي الله عنه told a man, "Shall I not give you as gift a ḥadīth with which you will rejoice."

The man replied, "Why not?"

Ibn 'Abbās رضي الله عنه said, "Recite Sūrah Tabārakalladhi Biyadihil Mulk and teach it to your household and all your children and the children of your house and your neighbours for it is 'The Protector and The Defender (or Sayyidina Ibn Abbās رضي الله عنه said) and it will plead with its Lord for its reciter and it will intercede for its reciter to protect him from the punishment of the Fire and to save its reciter from the punishment of the grave. Rasūlullāh صلى الله عليه وسلم has said, 'It is my heart's desire that this sūrah be present in the heart of every person of my Ummah'." (Tha'labī)

Sūrah Al-Mulk

بِسْمِ اللّٰهِ الرَّحْمٰنِ الرَّحِيْمِ

In the name of Allāh, the Beneficent, the Merciful.

تَبٰرَكَ الَّذِىْ بِيَدِهِ الْمُلْكُ ۡ وَهُوَ عَلٰى كُلِّ شَىْءٍ قَدِيْرُ ۙ ﴿١﴾

Glorious is the One in whose hand is the Kingdom (of the whole universe), and He is powerful over everything,

الَّذِىْ خَلَقَ الْمَوْتَ وَالْحَيٰوةَ لِيَبْلُوَكُمْ اَيُّكُمْ اَحْسَنُ عَمَلًا ؕ وَهُوَ الْعَزِيْزُ الْغَفُوْرُ ۙ ﴿٢﴾

the One who created death and life, so that He may test you as to which of you is better in his deeds. And He is the All-Mighty, the Most-Forgiving,

الَّذِىْ خَلَقَ سَبْعَ سَمٰوٰتٍ طِبَاقًا ؕ مَا تَرٰى فِىْ خَلْقِ الرَّحْمٰنِ مِنْ تَفٰوُتٍ

ؕ فَارْجِعِ الْبَصَرَ ۙ هَلْ تَرٰى مِنْ فُطُوْرٍ ﴿٣﴾

who has created seven skies, one over the other. You will see nothing out of proportion in the creation of the Raḥmān (the All-Merciful Allāh). So, cast your eye again. Do you see any rifts?

ثُمَّ ارْجِعِ الْبَصَرَ كَرَّتَيْنِ يَنْقَلِبْ اِلَيْكَ الْبَصَرُ خَاسِئًا وَّهُوَ حَسِيْرٌ ﴿٤﴾

Then cast your eye again and again, and the eye will come back to you abased, in a state of weariness.

DATE:	✓	R

وَلَقَدْ زَيَّنَّا السَّمَآءَ الدُّنْيَا بِمَصَابِيْحَ وَجَعَلْنٰهَا رُجُوْمًا لِّلشَّيٰطِيْنِ وَاَعْتَدْنَا لَهُمْ عَذَابَ السَّعِيْرِ ﴿۵﴾

And We have decorated the nearest sky with lamps, and have made them devices to stone the devils, and We have prepared for them the punishment of Hell.

وَلِلَّذِيْنَ كَفَرُوْا بِرَبِّهِمْ عَذَابُ جَهَنَّمَ ؕ وَبِئْسَ الْمَصِيْرُ ﴿۶﴾

And for those who disbelieved in their Lord, there is the punishment of Jahannam, and it is an evil end.

اِذَآ اُلْقُوْا فِيْهَا سَمِعُوْا لَهَا شَهِيْقًا وَّهِيَ تَفُوْرُ ۙ ﴿۷﴾

When they will be thrown in it, they will hear a terrible sound from it, and it will be boiling,

تَكَادُ تَمَيَّزُ مِنَ الْغَيْظِ ؕ كُلَّمَآ اُلْقِيَ فِيْهَا فَوْجٌ سَاَلَهُمْ خَزَنَتُهَآ اَلَمْ يَاْتِكُمْ نَذِيْرٌ ﴿۸﴾

seeming as if it will burst out of fury. Whenever a group is thrown into it, its keepers will say to them, "Had no warner come to you?"

قَالُوْا بَلٰى قَدْ جَآءَنَا نَذِيْرٌ ۙ۬ فَكَذَّبْنَا وَقُلْنَا مَا نَزَّلَ اللّٰهُ مِنْ شَيْءٍ ۚۖ اِنْ اَنْتُمْ اِلَّا فِيْ ضَلٰلٍ كَبِيْرٍ ﴿۹﴾

They will say, "Yes, a warner had come to us, but We had rejected, and said, 'Allāh has not revealed anything. You are only in great error.'"

وَقَالُوْا لَوْ كُنَّا نَسْمَعُ اَوْ نَعْقِلُ مَا كُنَّا فِيْۤ اَصْحٰبِ السَّعِيْرِ ﴿۱۰﴾

And they will say, "Had we been listening or understanding, we would not have been among the people of the Hell."

DATE:	✓	R

Sūrah Al-Mulk

فَاعْتَرَفُوا بِذَنْبِهِمْ ۚ فَسُحْقًا لِّأَصْحَابِ السَّعِيرِ ١١

Thus they will confess their sin. So, away with the people of the Hell!

إِنَّ الَّذِينَ يَخْشَوْنَ رَبَّهُم بِالْغَيْبِ لَهُم مَّغْفِرَةٌ وَأَجْرٌ كَبِيرٌ ١٢

Surely, for those who have awe of their Lord without seeing (Him), there is forgiveness and a big reward.

وَأَسِرُّوا قَوْلَكُمْ أَوِ اجْهَرُوا بِهِ ۖ إِنَّهُ عَلِيمٌ بِذَاتِ الصُّدُورِ ١٣

Whether you keep your talk secret or make it aloud, He knows well what lies in the hearts.

أَلَا يَعْلَمُ مَنْ خَلَقَ ۖ وَهُوَ اللَّطِيفُ الْخَبِيرُ ١٤

Is it (imaginable) that He who has created (them) will not have (such a) knowledge, while He is the Knower of the finest things, the All-Aware?

هُوَ الَّذِي جَعَلَ لَكُمُ الْأَرْضَ ذَلُولًا فَامْشُوا فِي مَنَاكِبِهَا وَكُلُوا مِن رِّزْقِهِ ۖ وَإِلَيْهِ النُّشُورُ ١٥

He is the One who has made the earth subjugated for you, so walk on its shoulders, and eat out of His provision, and to Him is the Resurrection.

أَأَمِنتُم مَّن فِي السَّمَاءِ أَن يَخْسِفَ بِكُمُ الْأَرْضَ فَإِذَا هِيَ تَمُورُ ١٦

Have you become fearless of Him who is in the sky if He makes you sink into the earth, and it starts trembling at once?

DATE: ✓ R

أَمْ أَمِنْتُمْ مَّنْ فِى السَّمَآءِ أَنْ يُّرْسِلَ عَلَيْكُمْ حَاصِبًا ۗ فَسَتَعْلَمُوْنَ كَيْفَ نَذِيْرِ ۞

Or, have you become fearless of Him who is in the sky if He loosens a violent wind with stones against you? So, you will soon come to know how was My warning!

وَلَقَدْ كَذَّبَ الَّذِيْنَ مِنْ قَبْلِهِمْ فَكَيْفَ كَانَ نَكِيْرِ ۞

And of course, those before them (also) rejected (the truth). So, how was My punishment?

أَوَلَمْ يَرَوْا إِلَى الطَّيْرِ فَوْقَهُمْ صَفّٰتٍ وَّيَقْبِضْنَ ۚ

مَا يُمْسِكُهُنَّ إِلَّا الرَّحْمٰنُ ۚ إِنَّهُ بِكُلِّ شَىْءٍۢ بَصِيْرٌ ۞

Have they not looked to the birds above them spreading their wings, and (at times) they fold (them) in? No one holds them up except the Raḥmān (the All-Merciful Allāh). Surely He is watchful of every thing.

أَمَّنْ هٰذَا الَّذِىْ هُوَ جُنْدٌ لَّكُمْ يَنْصُرُكُمْ مِّنْ دُوْنِ الرَّحْمٰنِ ۚ إِنِ الْكٰفِرُوْنَ إِلَّا فِىْ غُرُوْرٍ ۞

Now, who is there to act as a force for you to help you, except the Raḥmān ? The disbelievers are in nothing but delusion.

أَمَّنْ هٰذَا الَّذِىْ يَرْزُقُكُمْ إِنْ أَمْسَكَ رِزْقَهُ ۚ بَلْ لَّجُّوْا فِىْ عُتُوٍّ وَّنُفُوْرٍ ۞

Or, who is there to give you sustenance, if He withholds His sustenance? Still, they persist in rebellion and aversion.

DATE: | ✓ | R

Sūrah Al-Mulk

أَفَمَن يَمْشِي مُكِبًّا عَلَىٰ وَجْهِهِۦٓ أَهْدَىٰٓ أَمَّن يَمْشِي سَوِيًّا عَلَىٰ صِرَٰطٍ مُّسْتَقِيمٍ ٢٢

Then, is the one who walks falling down (frequently) on his face more right or the one who walks properly on a straight path?

قُلْ هُوَ ٱلَّذِيٓ أَنشَأَكُمْ وَجَعَلَ لَكُمُ ٱلسَّمْعَ وَٱلْأَبْصَٰرَ وَٱلْأَفْـِٔدَةَ ۖ قَلِيلًا مَّا تَشْكُرُونَ ٢٣

Say, "He is the One who has originated you, and made for you ears and eyes and hearts. How little you pay gratitude!"

قُلْ هُوَ ٱلَّذِي ذَرَأَكُمْ فِي ٱلْأَرْضِ وَإِلَيْهِ تُحْشَرُونَ ٢٣

Say, "He is the One who has scattered you on the earth, and to Him you will be assembled."

وَيَقُولُونَ مَتَىٰ هَٰذَا ٱلْوَعْدُ إِن كُنتُمْ صَٰدِقِينَ ٢٥

And they say, "When will this promise (of the Day of Judgement) be fulfilled, if you are true?"

قُلْ إِنَّمَا ٱلْعِلْمُ عِندَ ٱللَّهِ وَإِنَّمَآ أَنَا۠ نَذِيرٌ مُّبِينٌ ٢٦

Say, "The knowledge (of that Day) is only with Allāh, and I am only a plain warner.

DATE:	✓	R

فَلَمَّا رَاَوْهُ زُلْفَةً سِيْٓءَتْ وُجُوْهُ الَّذِيْنَ كَفَرُوْا وَقِيْلَ هٰذَا الَّذِيْ كُنْتُمْ بِهٖ تَدَّعُوْنَ ۝

Then, once they will see it approaching, the faces of the disbelievers will be turned awkward, and it will be said, "This is what you were calling for!"

قُلْ اَرَءَيْتُمْ اِنْ اَهْلَكَنِيَ اللّٰهُ وَمَنْ مَّعِيَ اَوْ رَحِمَنَا فَمَنْ يُّجِيْرُ الْكٰفِرِيْنَ مِنْ عَذَابٍ اَلِيْمٍ ۝

Say, "Tell me, if Allāh destroys me and those who are with me (as you wish), or has mercy on us (as we wish), who can (in either case) save the disbelievers from a painful punishment?"

قُلْ هُوَ الرَّحْمٰنُ اٰمَنَّا بِهٖ وَعَلَيْهِ تَوَكَّلْنَا فَسَتَعْلَمُوْنَ مَنْ هُوَ فِيْ ضَلٰلٍ مُّبِيْنٍ ۝

Say, "He is the Raḥmān; we have believed in Him, and in Him we placed our trust. So, you will soon come to know who is in open error."

قُلْ اَرَءَيْتُمْ اِنْ اَصْبَحَ مَآؤُكُمْ غَوْرًا فَمَنْ يَّأْتِيْكُمْ بِمَآءٍ مَّعِيْنٍ ۝

Say, "Tell me, Should your water vanish into the earth, who will bring you a flowing (stream of) water?

DATE: ✓ R

The Virtues of Sūrah Al-Wāqi'ah

Sayyidina 'Uthmān رضي الله عنه went to Sayyidina Ibn Mas'ūd رضي الله عنه paying him a visit in his sickness from which he eventually passed away.

Sayyidina Ibn Mas'ūd رضي الله عنه said, "Do you fear poverty over my daughters, I have instructed them to recite Sūrah Wāqi'ah every night for I have heard Rasūlullāh صلى الله عليه وسلم say,

'He who recites Sūrah Wāqi'ah every night, poverty will never afflict him." (Bayhaqī, Ibn Kathīr)

Sūrah Al-Wāqi'ah

بِسْمِ اللّٰهِ الرَّحْمٰنِ الرَّحِيْمِ

In the name of Allāh, the Beneficent, the Merciful.

إِذَا وَقَعَتِ الْوَاقِعَةُ ﴿١﴾

When the Imminent Event (of Doom) will occur,

لَيْسَ لِوَقْعَتِهَا كَاذِبَةٌ ﴿٢﴾

there will be no one to deny its occurrence.

خَافِضَةٌ رَّافِعَةٌ ﴿٣﴾

It will be abasing (some), exalting (others)

إِذَا رُجَّتِ الْأَرْضُ رَجًّا ﴿٤﴾

when the Earth will be jolted with a terrible jolt,

وَّبُسَّتِ الْجِبَالُ بَسًّا ﴿٥﴾

and the mountains will be crumbled a thorough crumbling,

فَكَانَتْ هَبَآءً مُّنْبَثًّا ﴿٦﴾

until they will become dust, scattered in the air,

وَّكُنْتُمْ أَزْوَاجًا ثَلٰثَةً ﴿٧﴾

and you will be (divided into) three categories.

DATE:	✓	R

Sūrah Al-Wāqi'ah

فَأَصْحَٰبُ ٱلْمَيْمَنَةِ مَآ أَصْحَٰبُ ٱلْمَيْمَنَةِ ٨

As for the People of the Right, how (lucky) are the People of the Right!

وَأَصْحَٰبُ ٱلْمَشْـَٔمَةِ مَآ أَصْحَٰبُ ٱلْمَشْـَٔمَةِ ٩

And the People of the Left ? How (wretched) are the People of the Left!

وَٱلسَّٰبِقُونَ ٱلسَّٰبِقُونَ ١٠

And the Foremost are the foremost.

أُو۟لَٰٓئِكَ ٱلْمُقَرَّبُونَ ١١

Those are the ones blessed with nearness (to Allāh)

فِى جَنَّٰتِ ٱلنَّعِيمِ ١٢

in gardens of bliss,

ثُلَّةٌ مِّنَ ٱلْأَوَّلِينَ ١٣

many from the first generations,

وَقَلِيلٌ مِّنَ ٱلْءَاخِرِينَ ١٤

and a few from the later ones.

عَلَىٰ سُرُرٍ مَّوْضُونَةٍ ١٥

(They will be sitting) on thrones woven with gold,

DATE:	✓	R

Sūrah Al-Wāqi'ah

مُّتَّكِـِٔينَ عَلَيْهَا مُتَقَٰبِلِينَ ﴿١٦﴾

reclining on them, facing each other.

يَطُوفُ عَلَيْهِمْ وِلْدَٰنٌ مُّخَلَّدُونَ ﴿١٧﴾

Immortal boys will rotate around them

بِأَكْوَابٍ وَأَبَارِيقَ وَكَأْسٍ مِّن مَّعِينٍ ﴿١٨﴾

with bowls and jugs and a goblet of pure wine,

لَّا يُصَدَّعُونَ عَنْهَا وَلَا يُنزِفُونَ ﴿١٩﴾

from which they will neither suffer headache, nor will they be intoxicated,

وَفَٰكِهَةٍ مِّمَّا يَتَخَيَّرُونَ ﴿٢٠﴾

and with fruits that they choose,

وَلَحْمِ طَيْرٍ مِّمَّا يَشْتَهُونَ ﴿٢١﴾

and the flesh of birds that they desire.

وَحُورٌ عِينٌ ﴿٢٢﴾

And (for them there will be) ḥūrs, having lovely big eyes,

كَأَمْثَٰلِ ٱللُّؤْلُؤِ ٱلْمَكْنُونِ ﴿٢٣﴾

all (neat and clean) like a hidden pearl,

DATE: | ✓ | R

Sūrah Al-Wāqi'ah

جَزَآءًۢ بِمَا كَانُوْا يَعْمَلُوْنَ ۝

as a reward for what they used to do.

لَا يَسْمَعُوْنَ فِيْهَا لَغْوًا وَّلَا تَأْثِيْمًا ۝

They will hear neither an absurd talk in it, nor something leading to sin,

اِلَّا قِيْلًا سَلٰمًا سَلٰمًا ۝

but (they will hear) the words of salām, salām (as greetings).

وَاَصْحٰبُ الْيَمِيْنِ ۙ مَآ اَصْحٰبُ الْيَمِيْنِ ۝

And the People of the Right? How (lucky) are the People of the Right!

فِيْ سِدْرٍ مَّخْضُوْدٍ ۝

(They will be) amid lote-trees with no thorns,

وَّطَلْحٍ مَّنْضُوْدٍ ۝

and the trees of Ṭalḥ, (banana, or a fragrant tree) having layers one upon the other,

وَّظِلٍّ مَّمْدُوْدٍ ۝

and a shade, spread all over,

وَّمَآءٍ مَّسْكُوْبٍ ۝

and water, poured forth,

DATE: ✓ R

Sūrah Al-Wāqi'ah

وَّفَاكِهَةٍ كَثِيۡرَةٍ ۙ (٣٢)

and a lot of fruits,

لَّا مَقۡطُوۡعَةٍ وَّلَا مَمۡنُوۡعَةٍ ۙ (٣٣)

neither interrupted (in any season), nor prohibited,

وَّفُرُشٍ مَّرۡفُوۡعَةٍ ؕ (٣٤)

and mattresses of high quality.

اِنَّاۤ اَنۡشَاۡنٰهُنَّ اِنۡشَآءً ۙ (٣٥)

Surely We have made up those females in a special creation,

فَجَعَلۡنٰهُنَّ اَبۡكَارًا ۙ (٣٦)

and have made them virgins,

عُرُبًا اَتۡرَابًا ۙ (٣٧)

loving to their husbands, matching them in age,

لِّاَصۡحٰبِ الۡيَمِيۡنِ ؕ (٣٨)

for the People of the Right,

ثُلَّةٌ مِّنَ الۡاَوَّلِيۡنَ ۙ (٣٩)

(comprising) many from the first generations,

DATE:	✓	R

Sūrah Al-Wāqi'ah

وَثُلَّةٌ مِّنَ الْاٰخِرِيْنَ ﴿٣٠﴾

and many from the later ones.

وَاَصْحٰبُ الشِّمَالِ ۙ۬ مَآ اَصْحٰبُ الشِّمَالِ ﴿٣١﴾

And the People of the Left? How (wretched) are the People of the Left!

فِيْ سَمُوْمٍ وَّحَمِيْمٍ ﴿٣٢﴾

(They will be) in scorching wind and boiling water,

وَّظِلٍّ مِّنْ يَّحْمُوْمٍ ﴿٣٣﴾

and in a shade of black smoke,

لَّا بَارِدٍ وَّلَا كَرِيْمٍ ﴿٣٤﴾

neither cool nor graceful.

اِنَّهُمْ كَانُوْا قَبْلَ ذٰلِكَ مُتْرَفِيْنَ ﴿٣٥﴾

They were earlier in luxuries,

وَكَانُوْا يُصِرُّوْنَ عَلَى الْحِنْثِ الْعَظِيْمِ ﴿٣٦﴾

and used to persist in major sins,

وَكَانُوْا يَقُوْلُوْنَ ۙ۬ اَىِٕذَا مِتْنَا وَكُنَّا تُرَابًا وَّعِظَامًا ءَاِنَّا لَمَبْعُوْثُوْنَ ﴿٣٧﴾

and used to say, "Is it that when we die and become dust - is it that we will be raised again,

DATE: | ✓ | R

اَوَ اٰبَآؤُنَا الْاَوَّلُوْنَ ۟

and our ancient fathers as well?"

قُلْ اِنَّ الْاَوَّلِيْنَ وَ الْاٰخِرِيْنَ ۟

Say, "All the earlier and the later ones

لَمَجْمُوْعُوْنَ ۙ اِلٰى مِيْقَاتِ يَوْمٍ مَّعْلُوْمٍ ۟

will be gathered together for a fixed time of a specified day.

ثُمَّ اِنَّكُمْ اَيُّهَا الضَّآلُّوْنَ الْمُكَذِّبُوْنَ ۟

Then O you, the erring, the denying people,

لَاٰكِلُوْنَ مِنْ شَجَرٍ مِّنْ زَقُّوْمٍ ۟

you will have to eat from the Tree of Zaqqūm,

فَمَالِئُوْنَ مِنْهَا الْبُطُوْنَ ۟

and to fill with it the bellies,

فَشٰرِبُوْنَ عَلَيْهِ مِنَ الْحَمِيْمِ ۟

then on top of it you will have to drink boiling water,

فَشٰرِبُوْنَ شُرْبَ الْهِيْمِ ۟

and to drink like camels suffering from the disease of over-thirst.

DATE: ✓ R

هَٰذَا نُزُلُهُمْ يَوْمَ الدِّينِ ٥٦

This will be their welcome entertainment on the Day of Judgement.

نَحْنُ خَلَقْنَاكُمْ فَلَوْلَا تُصَدِّقُونَ ٥٧

We have created you; then why do you not believe in it?

أَفَرَأَيْتُمْ مَا تُمْنُونَ ٥٨

So, tell Me about the semen you drop (in the wombs):

أَأَنْتُمْ تَخْلُقُونَهُ أَمْ نَحْنُ الْخَالِقُونَ ٥٩

Is it you who create it, or are We the Creator?

نَحْنُ قَدَّرْنَا بَيْنَكُمُ الْمَوْتَ وَمَا نَحْنُ بِمَسْبُوقِينَ ٦٠

We have appointed (the times of) death among you, and We cannot be frustrated

عَلَىٰ أَنْ نُبَدِّلَ أَمْثَالَكُمْ وَنُنْشِئَكُمْ فِي مَا لَا تَعْلَمُونَ ٦١

from replacing you with others like you, and creating you (afresh) in that (form) which you do not know.

وَلَقَدْ عَلِمْتُمُ النَّشْأَةَ الْأُولَىٰ فَلَوْلَا تَذَكَّرُونَ ٦٢

And you certainly know the first creation; then why do you not take lesson?

أَفَرَأَيْتُمْ مَا تَحْرُثُونَ ٦٣

Well, tell Me about that (seed) which you sow:

DATE:	✓	R

ءَاَنۡتُمۡ تَزۡرَعُوۡنَهٗٓ اَمۡ نَحۡنُ الزّٰرِعُوۡنَ ۞

Is it you who grow it, or are We the One who grows?

لَوۡ نَشَآءُ لَجَعَلۡنٰهُ حُطَامًا فَظَلۡتُمۡ تَفَكَّهُوۡنَ ۞

If We so will, We can certainly make it crumbled, and you will remain wondering,

اِنَّا لَمُغۡرَمُوۡنَ ۞

(and saying,) "We are laden with debt,

بَلۡ نَحۡنُ مَحۡرُوۡمُوۡنَ ۞

rather we are totally deprived."

اَفَرَءَيۡتُمُ الۡمَآءَ الَّذِىۡ تَشۡرَبُوۡنَ ۞

Again, tell Me about the water you drink:

ءَاَنۡتُمۡ اَنۡزَلۡتُمُوۡهُ مِنَ الۡمُزۡنِ اَمۡ نَحۡنُ الۡمُنۡزِلُوۡنَ ۞

Is it you who have brought it down from the clouds, or are We the One who sends (it) down?

لَوۡ نَشَآءُ جَعَلۡنٰهُ اُجَاجًا فَلَوۡلَا تَشۡكُرُوۡنَ ۞

If We so will, We can make it bitter in taste. So why do you not offer gratitude?

اَفَرَءَيۡتُمُ النَّارَ الَّتِىۡ تُوۡرُوۡنَ ۞

Now tell Me about the fire you kindle:

DATE: ✓ R

Sūrah Al-Wāqi'ah

ءَاَنْتُمْ اَنْشَاْتُمْ شَجَرَتَهَآ اَمْ نَحْنُ الْمُنْشِئُوْنَ ۝

Is it you who have originated its tree, or are We the Originator?

نَحْنُ جَعَلْنٰهَا تَذْكِرَةً وَّمَتَاعًا لِّلْمُقْوِيْنَ ۝

We have made it a reminder (of Our infinite power, and of the fire of Hell) and a benefit for travellers in deserts.

فَسَبِّحْ بِاسْمِ رَبِّكَ الْعَظِيْمِ ۝

So, proclaim purity of the name of your Lord, the Magnificent.

فَلَاۤ اُقْسِمُ بِمَوٰقِعِ النُّجُوْمِ ۝

So, I swear by the setting places of the stars,

وَاِنَّهٗ لَقَسَمٌ لَّوْ تَعْلَمُوْنَ عَظِيْمٌ ۝

and indeed it is a great oath, if you are to appreciate

اِنَّهٗ لَقُرْاٰنٌ كَرِيْمٌ ۝

it is surely the Noble Qur'ān,

فِيْ كِتٰبٍ مَّكْنُوْنٍ ۝

(recorded already) in a protected book (i.e. the Preserved Tablet)

لَّا يَمَسُّهٗۤ اِلَّا الْمُطَهَّرُوْنَ ۝

that is not touched except by the purified ones (the angels).

DATE: ☑ R

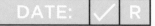

Sūrah Al-Wāqi'ah

تَنۡزِيۡلٌ مِّنۡ رَّبِّ الۡعٰلَمِيۡنَ ﴿٨٠﴾

a revelation from the Lord of the worlds.

اَفَبِهٰذَا الۡحَدِيۡثِ اَنۡتُمۡ مُّدۡهِنُوۡنَ ﴿٨١﴾

Is it this discourse that you take lightly,

وَتَجۡعَلُوۡنَ رِزۡقَكُمۡ اَنَّكُمۡ تُكَذِّبُوۡنَ ﴿٨٢﴾

and take your denial as your livelihood?

فَلَوۡلَاۤ اِذَا بَلَغَتِ الۡحُلۡقُوۡمَ ﴿٨٣﴾

So why (do you) not (intervene) when the soul (of a dying person) reaches the throat,

وَاَنۡتُمۡ حِيۡنَـئِذٍ تَنۡظُرُوۡنَ ﴿٨٣﴾

and you are watching?

وَنَحۡنُ اَقۡرَبُ اِلَيۡهِ مِنۡكُمۡ وَلٰـكِنۡ لَّا تُبۡصِرُوۡنَ ﴿٨٥﴾

And We are closer to him than you, but you do not perceive.

DATE: | ✓ | R

Sūrah Al-Wāqi'ah

فَلَوْلَآ اِنْ كُنْتُمْ غَيْرَ مَدِيْنِيْنَ ۙ ٨٢

So, if you are not going to be recompensed (in the Hereafter for your deeds), then why do you not

تَرْجِعُوْنَهَآ اِنْ كُنْتُمْ صٰدِقِيْنَ ۚ ٨٧

bring the soul back, if you are truthful?

فَاَمَّآ اِنْ كَانَ مِنَ الْمُقَرَّبِيْنَ ۙ ٨٨

So, in case he (the dying person) is from among those blessed with nearness,

فَرَوْحٌ وَّرَيْحَانٌ ۙ وَّجَنَّتُ نَعِيْمٍ ٨٩

then (for him) there is comfort and fragrance and garden of bliss.

وَاَمَّآ اِنْ كَانَ مِنْ اَصْحٰبِ الْيَمِيْنِ ۙ ٩٠

And in case he is from among the People of the Right,

فَسَلٰمٌ لَّكَ مِنْ اَصْحٰبِ الْيَمِيْنِ ۚ ٩١

then, (it will be said to him,) "Peace is for you, as you are one of the People of the Right."

DATE: ✓ R

Sūrah Al-Wāqi'ah

وَأَمَّآ إِن كَانَ مِنَ ٱلْمُكَذِّبِينَ ٱلضَّآلِّينَ ٩٢

But if he is one of the deniers, the astray,

فَنُزُلٌ مِّنْ حَمِيمٍ ٩٣

then (for him) there is entertainment from boiling water,

وَتَصْلِيَةُ جَحِيمٍ ٩٤

and burning in the Hell.

إِنَّ هَٰذَا لَهُوَ حَقُّ ٱلْيَقِينِ ٩٥

Indeed this is certainty in its true sense.

فَسَبِّحْ بِٱسْمِ رَبِّكَ ٱلْعَظِيمِ ٩٦

So, proclaim purity of the name of your Lord, the Magnificent.

DATE:	✓	R

F1
Du'ā'

The first Kalimah

لَا إِلٰهَ إِلَّا اللّٰهُ مُحَمَّدٌ رَّسُوْلُ اللّٰهِ

There is none worthy of worship but Allāh, (and) Muḥammad is the messenger of Allāh.

DATE:	✓	R

Before starting anything

بِسْمِ اللّٰهِ

I begin in the name of Allāh
(Kitāb al-Adhkār)

DATE:	✓	R

After completing anything

اَلْحَمْدُ لِلّٰهِ

Praise be to Allāh.
(Kitāb al-Adhkār)

DATE:	✓	R

When we want to do something

إِنْ شَاءَ اللّٰهُ

If Allāh wills.
(Sūrah Al-Kahf)

DATE: | ✓ | R

When someone gives us something

جَزَاكَ اللّٰهُ خَيْرًا

May Allāh reward you with goodness.
(Tirmidhī)

DATE: | ✓ | R

When we see something nice

مَا شَاءَ اللّٰهُ

As Allāh wishes.
(Sūrah Al-Kahf)

DATE: | ✓ | R

When we see something great

سُبْحَانَ اللّٰهِ

Allāh is perfect.
(Ṣaḥīḥ Muslim)

DATE:	✓	R

When we climb up the stairs

اَللّٰهُ اَكْبَرُ

Allāh is the greatest.
(Ṣaḥīḥ al-Bukhārī)

DATE:	✓	R

When we go down the stairs

سُبْحَانَ اللّٰه

Allāh is perfect.
(Ṣaḥīḥ al-Bukhārī)

DATE:	✓	R

When we make a mistake we say:

اَسْتَغْفِرُ اللّٰهَ

I Ask forgiveness from Allāh.
(Ṣaḥīḥ al-Bukhārī)

DATE:	✓	R

Ta'awwudh

أَعُوْذُ بِاللّٰهِ مِنَ الشَّيْطَانِ الرَّجِيْمِ

I seek refuge with Allāh from Shayṭān, the accursed one.

DATE:	✓	R

At the time of eating

بِسْمِ اللّٰهِ وَبَرَكَةِ اللّٰهِ

With the name of Allāh and the blessings of Allāh. (Ḥākim)

DATE:	✓	R

At the time of sleeping

اَللّٰهُمَّ بِاسْمِكَ أَمُوْتُ وَأَحْيٰ

O Allāh, With Your name I die and live. (Ṣaḥīḥ al-Bukhārī)

DATE:	✓	R

When greeting a Muslim

اَلسَّلَامُ عَلَيْكُمْ وَرَحْمَةُ اللّٰهِ وَبَرَكَاتُهُ

May the peace, mercy, and blessings of Allāh be upon you. (Abū Dāwūd)

DATE:	✓	R

Reply to the salām

وَعَلَيْكُمُ السَّلَامُ وَرَحْمَةُ اللهِ وَبَرَكَاتُهُ

And peace, mercy and blessings of Allāh be upon you (too).
(Musnad Aḥmad)

DATE: | ✓ | R

At the time of drinking water

بِسْمِ اللهِ الرَّحْمٰنِ الرَّحِيْمِ

I begin in the name of Allāh, who is the Most Merciful, Most Gracious.
(Ṣaḥīḥ al-Bukhārī)

DATE: | ✓ | R

After drinking water

اَلْحَمْدُ لِلّٰهِ

Praise be to Allāh.
(Ṣaḥīḥ Muslim)

DATE: | ✓ | R

F2
Du'ā'

The second Kalimah

أَشْهَدُ أَنْ لَّآ إِلٰهَ إِلَّا اللّٰهُ وَأَشْهَدُ أَنَّ مُحَمَّدًا

عَبْدُهٗ وَرَسُوْلُهٗ

I bear witness that (there is) no God except Allāh and I bear witness that Muḥammad is His Servant and Messenger.
(Ṣaḥīḥ al-Bukhārī)

DATE: ✓ R

The third Kalimah

سُبْحَانَ اللّٰهِ وَالْحَمْدُ لِلّٰهِ وَلَآ إِلٰهَ إِلَّا اللّٰهُ وَاللّٰهُ أَكْبَرُ وَلَا حَوْلَ

وَلَا قُوَّةَ إِلَّا بِاللّٰهِ الْعَلِيِّ الْعَظِيْمِ

Exalted is Allāh, and praise be to Allāh, and there is no God except Allāh, and Allāh is the Greatest. And there is no might nor power except in Allāh, the Most High, the Most Great.
(Abū Dāwūd)

DATE: ✓ R

When we hear our Messenger صلى الله عليه وسلم's name

صَلَّى اللّٰهُ عَلَيْهِ وَسَلَّمْ

May Allāh's mercy and peace be upon him.
(Tirmidhī)

DATE:	✓	R

When we lose something

اِنَّا لِلّٰهِ وَإِنَّا إِلَيْهِ رَاجِعُوْنَ

To Allāh we belong and to Him do we all return.
(Sūrah Al-Baqarah)

DATE:	✓	R

When we are frightened

أَعُوْذُ بِاللّٰهِ

I seek protection with Allāh.
(Sūrah Fuṣṣilat)

DATE:	✓	R

When we sneeze

ٱلْحَمْدُ لِلّٰهِ

All praise belongs to Allāh.
(Ṣaḥīḥ al-Bukhārī)

DATE:	✓	R

When another person sneezes

يَرْحَمُكَ اللّٰهُ

May Allāh have mercy on you.
(Ṣaḥīḥ al-Bukhārī)

DATE:	✓	R

The reply of the sneezing person

يَهْدِيكُمُ اللّٰهُ وَيُصْلِحُ بَالَكُمْ

May Allah guide you and grant you well-being.
(Ṣaḥīḥ al-Bukhārī)

DATE:	✓	R

When entering the washroom

اَللّٰهُمَّ إِنِّيْ أَعُوْذُبِكَ مِنَ الْخُبُثِ وَالْخَبَائِثِ

O Allāh, I seek refuge in you from all evil and evil doers.
(Ṣaḥīḥ al-Bukhārī)

DATE:	✓	R

When leaving the washroom

غُفْرَانَكَ

اَلْحَمْدُ لِلّٰهِ الَّذِيْ أَذْهَبَ عَنِّي الْأَذٰى وَعَافَانِيْ

O Allāh. I seek your forgiveness. All praises are due to Allāh who has taken away from me discomfort and granted me comfort.
(Abū Dāwūd)

DATE:	✓	R

After eating

اَلْحَمْدُ لِلّٰهِ الَّذِيْ أَطْعَمَنَا وَسَقَانَا وَجَعَلَنَا مُسْلِمِيْنَ

All praise is due to Allāh, who gave us food and drink and made us Muslims.
(Abū Dāwūd)

DATE:	✓	R

When we forget to recite the du'ā' at the time of eating

بِسْمِ اللّٰهِ أَوَّلَهُ وَآخِرَهُ

With the name of Allāh in the beginning and the end.
(Abū Dāwūd)

DATE:	✓	R

When drinking milk

اَللّٰهُمَّ بَارِكْ لَنَا فِيْهِ وَزِدْنَا مِنْهُ

O Allāh, grant us blessings in it and grant us more of it.
(Ibn Mājah)

DATE:	✓	R

When waking up

اَلْحَمْدُ لِلّٰهِ الَّذِيْ أَحْيَانَا بَعْدَ مَا أَمَاتَنَا وَإِلَيْهِ النُّشُوْرُ

All praise to Allāh, who gave us life after having given us death and to Him is our final return.
(Musnad Aḥmad)

DATE:	✓	R

C1
Du'ā'

The fourth Kalimah

لَا اِلٰهَ اِلَّا اللّٰهُ وَحْدَهٗ لَا شَرِيْكَ لَهٗ، لَهُ الْمُلْكُ وَلَهُ الْحَمْدُ يُحْيِ وَيُمِيْتُ بِيَدِهِ

الْخَيْرُ وَهُوَ عَلٰى كُلِّ شَيْءٍ قَدِيْرٌ

There is none worthy of worship but Allāh, He is alone and He has no partner. For Him is the Kingdom and for Him is praise. He gives life and death. With Him is all good and He has power over all things.

(Bayhaqī)

DATE:	✓	R

The fifth Kalimah

اَللّٰهُمَّ اِنِّيْ اَعُوْذُبِكَ مِنْ اَنْ اُشْرِكَ بِكَ شَيْئًا وَّاَنَا اَعْلَمُ بِهٖ

وَاَسْتَغْفِرُكَ لِمَا لَا اَعْلَمُ بِهٖ تُبْتُ عَنْهُ وَتَبَرَّأْتُ مِنَ الْكُفْرِ وَالشِّرْكِ

وَالْمَعَاصِيْ كُلِّهَا اَسْلَمْتُ وَاَقُوْلُ لَا اِلٰهَ اِلَّا اللّٰهُ مُحَمَّدٌ رَّسُوْلُ اللّٰهِ

Oh Allāh I seek protection in You that I should join any partner with You knowingly. I seek Your forgiveness from that which I do not know. I repent from ignorance. I free myself from disbelief and from joining partners with You and (I free myself from) all sins. I submit to Your will. I believe and I declare: there is none worthy of worship besides Allāh and Muḥammad صلى الله عليه وسلم is the messenger of Allāh.

DATE:	✓	R

Takbīr Taḥrīmah

اَللهُ أَكْبَرُ

Allāh is the greatest.
(Tirmidhī)

DATE:	✓	R

Du'ā' al-Istiftāḥ

سُبْحَانَكَ اللّٰهُمَّ وَبِحَمْدِكَ وَتَبَارَكَ اسْمُكَ وَتَعَالٰى

جَدُّكَ وَلَا إِلٰهَ غَيْرُكَ

Perfect you are O Allāh and all praise is due to You, blessed is Your name and high is Your majesty. There is none worthy of worship other than You.
(Abū Dāwūd)

DATE:	✓	R

Tasbīḥ of rukū'

سُبْحَانَ رَبِّيَ الْعَظِيْمِ

Free from all defects is my Lord.
(Tirmidhī)

DATE:	✓	R

Rising from rukū'

سَمِعَ اللّٰهُ لِمَنْ حَمِدَهٗ

Allāh has heard he who praised him.
(Tirmidhī)

DATE:	✓	R

In Qawmah

رَبَّنَا وَلَكَ الْحَمْدُ

Our Lord, all praise is due only to You.
(Tirmidhī)

DATE:	✓	R

Tasbīḥ of sajdah

سُبْحَانَ رَبِّيَ الْاَعْلٰى

Perfect is my Great Sustainer, Most High.
(Tirmidhī)

DATE:	✓	R

Between the two sajdah

اَللّٰهُمَّ اغْفِرْ لِيْ وَارْحَمْنِيْ

O Allāh forgive me and have mercy on me.
(Ṣaḥīḥ Muslim)

DATE:	✓	R

Completing the ṣalāh

اَلسَّلَامُ عَلَيْكُمْ وَرَحْمَةُ اللّٰهِ

Peace and Allāh's mercy be upon you.

(Tirmidhī)

DATE:	✓	R

To increase ones knowledge

رَّبِّ زِدْنِيْ عِلْمًا

O my lord increase me in knowledge.

(Sūrah Ṭā Hā)

DATE:	✓	R

C2
Du'ā'

The sixth Kalimah - Īmān Mujmal

اٰمَنْتُ بِاللّٰهِ كَمَا هُوَ بِاَسْمَآئِهٖ وَصِفَاتِهٖ وَقَبِلْتُ جَمِيْعَ اَحْكَامِهٖ

I believe in Allāh as He is understood by His names and His attributes (qualities) and I accept all His orders.

DATE:	✓	R

The seventh Kalimah - Īmān Mufaṣṣal

اٰمَنْتُ بِاللّٰهِ وَمَلٰٓئِكَتِهٖ وَكُتُبِهٖ وَرُسُلِهٖ وَالْيَوْمِ الْاٰخِرِ وَالْقَدْرِ

خَيْرِهٖ وَشَرِّهٖ مِنَ اللّٰهِ تَعَالٰى وَالْبَعْثِ بَعْدَ الْمَوْتِ

I believe in Allāh and His angels and His books and His messengers and the Last Day and that good and bad is all from Allāh the Most High, and I believe in the raising after death.

DATE:	✓	R

Tashahhud

اَلتَّحِيَّاتُ لِلّٰهِ وَالصَّلَوَاتُ وَالطَّيِّبَاتُ، اَلسَّلَامُ عَلَيْكَ أَيُّهَا النَّبِيُّ وَرَحْمَةُ اللهِ

وَبَرَكَاتُهُ، اَلسَّلَامُ عَلَيْنَا وَعَلٰى عِبَادِ اللهِ الصَّالِحِيْنَ، أَشْهَدُ أَنْ لَّآ إِلٰهَ إِلَّا اللهُ،

وَأَشْهَدُ أَنَّ مُحَمَّدًا عَبْدُهُ وَرَسُوْلُهُ

"Greetings, prayers and goodness belong to Allāh. Peace be on you, O Prophet and the mercy of Allāh and His blessings. Peace be on us and on the righteous servants of Allāh, I bear witness that there is no God but Allāh and I bear witness that Muḥammad صلى الله عليه وسلم is His servant and Messenger."
(Ṣaḥīḥ al-Bukhārī)

DATE:	✓	R

Durūd Ibrāhīm

اللّٰهُمَّ صَلِّ عَلٰى مُحَمَّدٍ، وَّعَلٰى اٰلِ مُحَمَّدٍ، كَمَا صَلَّيْتَ عَلٰى إِبْرَاهِيْمَ

وَعَلٰى آلِ إِبْرَاهِيْمَ، إِنَّكَ حَمِيْدٌ مَّجِيْدٌ، اَللّٰهُمَّ بَارِكْ عَلٰى مُحَمَّدٍ، وَّعَلٰى

اٰلِ مُحَمَّدٍ، كَمَا بَارَكْتَ عَلٰى إِبْرَاهِيْمَ، وَعَلٰى اٰلِ إِبْرَاهِيْمَ، إِنَّكَ حَمِيْدٌ

مَّجِيْدٌ

O Allāh, send prayers upon Muḥammad and the followers of Muḥammad, just as You sent prayers upon Ibrāhīm and upon the followers of Ibrāhīm. Indeed, You are full of praise and majesty. O Allāh, send blessings upon Muḥammad and upon the followers of Muḥammad, just as You sent blessings upon Ibrāhīm and upon the followers of Ibrāhīm, Indeed, You are full of praise and majesty. (Tirmidhī)

DATE:	✓	R

After Durūd Ibrāhīm

اَللّٰهُمَّ إِنِّيْ ظَلَمْتُ نَفْسِيْ ظُلْمًا كَثِيْرًا، وَلَا

يَغْفِرُ الذُّنُوْبَ إِلَّا أَنْتَ

فَاغْفِرْ لِيْ مَغْفِرَةً مِنْ عِنْدِكَ، وَارْحَمْنِيْ إِنَّكَ

أَنْتَ الْغَفُوْرُ الرَّحِيْمُ

O Allāh, I have greatly wronged myself and no one forgives sins but You. So, grant me forgiveness and have mercy on me. Surely, You are Forgiving, Merciful.
(Ṣaḥīḥ al-Bukhārī)

DATE:	✓	R

Before wuḍū'

بِسۡمِ اللهِ

In the name of Allāh.
(Abū Dāwūd)

DATE: ✓ R

During wuḍū'

اَللّٰهُمَّ اغۡفِرۡ لِيۡ ذَنۡبِيۡ وَوَسِّعۡ لِيۡ فِيۡ دَارِيۡ وَبَارِكۡ لِيۡ فِيۡ رِزۡقِيۡ

O Allāh, forgive my sin, widen my home and bless my livelihood.
(As-Sunan al-Kubrā)

DATE: ✓ R

After wuḍū'

اَللّٰهُمَّ اجۡعَلۡنِيۡ مِنَ التَّوَّابِيۡنَ وَاجۡعَلۡنِيۡ مِنَ الۡمُتَطَهِّرِيۡنَ

O Allāh, make me from amongst who are the repenters and among those who keep very clean.
(Tirmidhī)

DATE: ✓ R

Entering the masjid

اَللّٰهُمَّ افْتَحْ لِي أَبْوَابَ رَحْمَتِكَ

O Allāh, open for me the doors of Your mercy.
(Ṣaḥīḥ Muslim)

DATE:	✓	R

Leaving the masjid

اَللّٰهُمَّ إِنِّي أَسْأَلُكَ مِنْ فَضْلِكَ

O Allāh, I ask you of Your favour.
(Ṣaḥīḥ Muslim)

DATE:	✓	R

C3
Du'ā'

When you see someone smiling

أَضْحَكَ اللهُ سِنَّكَ

May Allāh keep you laughing forever (happy).
(Ṣaḥīḥ al-Bukhārī)

DATE: | ✓ | R

Du'ā' to make for our parents

رَّبِّ ارْحَمْهُمَا كَمَا رَبَّيَانِي صَغِيرًا

My Lord, have mercy upon them as they brought me up (when I was) small.
(Sūrah Al-Isrā')

DATE: | ✓ | R

Entering a house

اللَّهُمَّ إِنِّي أَسْأَلُكَ خَيْرَ الْمَوْلَجِ وَخَيْرَ الْمَخْرَجِ

بِسْمِ اللهِ وَلَجْنَا وَبِاسْمِ اللهِ خَرَجْنَا وَعَلَى اللهِ رَبِّنَا تَوَكَّلْنَا

O Allāh, I beg of You the blessing of entering and leaving. With Allāh's name do we enter and with Alláh's name do we leave, and upon Allāh, our Lord, do we rely.
(Abū Dāwūd)

DATE: | ✓ | R

Leaving a house

بِسْمِ اللهِ تَوَكَّلْتُ عَلَى اللهِ وَلَا حَوْلَ وَلَا قُوَّةَ إِلَّا بِاللهِ

In the name of Allāh, I depend on Allāh, and we do not have any power to do good deeds or to avoid evil deeds except with the help of Allāh.
(Abū Dāwūd)

DATE:	✓	R

Qunūt

اَللّٰهُمَّ إِنَّا نَسْتَعِيْنُكَ، وَنَسْتَغْفِرُكَ، وَنُؤْمِنُ بِكَ وَنَتَوَكَّلُ عَلَيْكَ وَ

نُثْنِيْ عَلَيْكَ الْخَيْرَ، وَنَشْكُرُكَ وَلَا نَكْفُرُكَ وَنَخْلَعُ وَنَتْرُكُ مَنْ

يَفْجُرُكَ، اَللّٰهُمَّ إِيَّاكَ نَعْبُدُ، وَلَكَ نُصَلِّيْ وَنَسْجُدُ، وَإِلَيْكَ نَسْعٰى وَنَحْفِدُ

، نَرْجُوْا رَحْمَتَكَ، وَنَخْشٰى عَذَابَكَ، إِنَّ عَذَابَكَ بِالْكُفَّارِ مُلْحِقٌ

O Allāh, we seek Your aid and ask Your pardon, we believe in You and place our trust in You. We praise You with all good, thank You and do not disbelieve in You. We free ourselves and leave the one who rebels against You. O Allāh, it is You we worship, and unto You we pray and prostrate, and towards You we hasten and You we serve, we hope for Your mercy and fear Your punishment, verily Your punishment will fall upon the disbelievers.
(Muṣannaf ibn Abī Shaybah)

DATE:	✓	R

When wearing clothes

اَلْحَمْدُ لِلّٰهِ الَّذِىْ كَسَانِىْ مَا أُوَارِىْ بِهٖ عَوْرَتِىْ وَأَتَجَمَّلُ بِهٖ فِىْ حَيَاتِىْ

All praises are due to Allāh, who clothed me with which I cover my body and with which I adorn myself in my life.

(Tirmidhī)

DATE:	✓	R

When taking clothes off

بِسْمِ اللّٰهِ الَّذِىْ لَا إِلٰهَ إِلَّا هُوَ

In the name of Allāh, apart from whom there is no Lord.

(Ibnus Sunnī)

DATE:	✓	R

Du'ā' to make for the host

اَللّٰهُمَّ أَطْعِمْ مَنْ أَطْعَمَنِىْ وَاسْقِ مَنْ سَقَانِىْ

O Allāh, feed those who have fed me and fill those who have filled me.

(Musnad Aḥmad)

DATE:	✓	R

When breaking the fast

اَللّٰهُمَّ لَكَ صُمْتُ وَعَلٰى رِزْقِكَ اَفْطَرْتُ

O Allāh! I fasted for You and I break my fast with Your sustenance.
(Abū Dāwūd)

DATE:	✓	R

After the Ifṭār

ذَهَبَ الظَّمَأُ وَابْتَلَّتِ الْعُرُوْقُ، وَثَبَتَ الْأَجْرُ إِنْ شَاءَ اللّٰهُ

The thirst is gone, the veins are moistened and the reward is confirmed, if Allāh (Ta'ālā) wills.
(Abū Dāwūd)

DATE:	✓	R

When eating at someone's house

أَفْطَرَ عِنْدَكُمُ الصَّائِمُوْنَ وَأَكَلَ طَعَامَكُمُ الْأَبْرَارُ، وَصَلَّتْ عَلَيْكُمُ الْمَلَائِكَةُ

May the fasting (people) break their fast in your home, and may the dutiful and pious eat your food, and may the angels send prayers upon you.
(Abū Dāwūd)

DATE:	✓	R

When travelling

سُبْحَانَ الَّذِي سَخَّرَ لَنَا هٰذَا وَمَا كُنَّا لَهُ مُقْرِنِيْنَ وَإِنَّا إِلٰى رَبِّنَا لَمُنْقَلِبُوْنَ

Glory be to Him who has brought this under our control whereas we were unable to control it. Surely we are to return to Him.
(Ṣaḥīḥ Muslim)

DATE:	✓	R

When it rains

اَللّٰهُمَّ اجْعَلْهُ صَيِّبًا نَّافِعًا

O Allāh, make it beneficial rain.
(Nasa'ī)

DATE:	✓	R

When looking in the mirror

اَللّٰهُمَّ كَمَا أَحْسَنْتَ خَلْقِيْ، فَحَسِّنْ خُلُقِيْ

O Allah You have made my creation perfect, so make my character also the best.
(Musnad Aḥmad)

DATE:	✓	R

C4
Du'ā'

Āyatul Kursiy

ٱللَّهُ لَآ إِلَٰهَ إِلَّا هُوَ ٱلْحَىُّ ٱلْقَيُّومُ ۚ لَا تَأْخُذُهُۥ سِنَةٌ وَلَا نَوْمٌ ۚ لَّهُۥ مَا فِى

ٱلسَّمَٰوَٰتِ وَمَا فِى ٱلْأَرْضِ ۗ مَن ذَا ٱلَّذِى يَشْفَعُ عِندَهُۥٓ إِلَّا بِإِذْنِهِۦ ۚ

يَعْلَمُ مَا بَيْنَ أَيْدِيهِمْ وَمَا خَلْفَهُمْ ۖ وَلَا يُحِيطُونَ بِشَىْءٍ مِّنْ عِلْمِهِۦٓ إِلَّا

بِمَا شَآءَ ۚ وَسِعَ كُرْسِيُّهُ ٱلسَّمَٰوَٰتِ وَٱلْأَرْضَ ۖ وَلَا يَـُٔودُهُۥ حِفْظُهُمَا ۚ

وَهُوَ ٱلْعَلِىُّ ٱلْعَظِيمُ

Allāh: There is none worthy of worhip but Him, the Living, the All-Sustaining. Neither dozing overtakes Him nor sleep. To Him belongs all that is in the Heavens and all that is on the Earth. Who can intercede with Him without His permission? He knows what is before them and what is behind them; while they encompass nothing of His knowledge, except what He wills. His Kursiy (Chair) extends to the Heavens and to the Earth, and it does not weary Him to look after them. He is the All-High, the Supreme.
(Sūrah Al-Baqarah)

DATE:	✓	R

Adhān (call to prayer)

اَللهُ أَكْبَرُ اَللهُ أَكْبَرُ

"Allāh is the greatest, Allāh is the greatest"

اَللهُ أَكْبَرُ اَللهُ أَكْبَرُ

"Allāh is the greatest, Allāh is the greatest"

أَشْهَدُ أَنْ لَّآ إِلٰهَ إِلَّا اللهُ

"I bear witness that there none worthy of worship except God"

أَشْهَدُ أَنْ لَّآ إِلٰهَ إِلَّا اللهُ

"I bear witness that there none worthy of worship except God"

أَشْهَدُ أَنَّ مُحَمَّدًا رَسُوْلُ اللهِ

"I bear witness that Muḥammad is the Messenger of God"

أَشْهَدُ أَنَّ مُحَمَّدًا رَسُوْلُ اللهِ

"I bear witness that Muḥammad is the Messenger of God"

حَيَّ عَلَى الصَّلَاةِ

"Come to prayer"

حَيَّ عَلَى الصَّلَاةِ

"Come to prayer"

حَيَّ عَلَى الْفَلَاحِ

"Come to success

حَيَّ عَلَى الْفَلَاحِ

"Come to felicity"

اَللهُ أَكْبَرُ اَللهُ أَكْبَرُ

"Allāh is the greatest, Allāh is the greatest"

لَا إِلٰهَ إِلَّا اللهُ

"There is none worthy of worship except God"

DATE:	✓	R

(Ṣaḥīḥ Muslim)

Extra words for the adhān of Fajr

In Fajr adhān recite these words after حَيَّ عَلَى الْفَلَاح

الصَّلَاةُ خَيْرٌ مِّنَ النَّوْمِ ، الصَّلَاةُ خَيْرٌ مِّنَ النَّوْمِ

Prayer is better than sleep, prayer is better than sleep
(Ibn Majah)

DATE:	✓	R

Reply to the words of adhān

When the words حَيَّ عَلَى الْفَلَاح and حَيَّ عَلَى الصَّلَاة are said, say:

لَا حَوْلَ وَلَا قُوَّةَ إِلَّا بِاللهِ

There is no power or might except Allāh
(An-Nasa'ī)

DATE:	✓	R

After adhān

اللّٰهُمَّ رَبَّ هٰذِهِ الدَّعْوَةِ التَّامَّةِ وَالصَّلَاةِ

الْقَائِمَةِ اٰتِ مُحَمَّدًا الْوَسِيْلَةَ وَالْفَضِيْلَةَ وَابْعَثْهُ

مَقَامًا مَّحْمُوْدًا الَّذِيْ وَعَدْتَّهُ

O Allāh, Owner of this perfect call and Owner of this prayer to be performed, bestow upon Muḥammad al-wasīlah and al-fadīlah and raise him upon a praised platform which You have promised him. (Ṣaḥīḥ al-Bukhārī)

DATE	✓	R

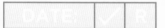

Janāzah du'ā'

اَللّٰهُمَّ اغْفِرْ لِحَيِّنَا وَمَيِّتِنَا، وَشَاهِدِنَا وَغَائِبِنَا، وَصَغِيْرِنَا

وَكَبِيْرِنَا، وَذَكَرِنَا وَأُنْثَانَا، اَللّٰهُمَّ مَنْ أَحْيَيْتَهُ مِنَّا فَأَحْيِهِ عَلَى

الْإِسْلَامِ، وَمَنْ تَوَفَّيْتَهُ مِنَّا فَتَوَفَّهُ عَلَى الْإِيْمَانِ، اَللّٰهُمَّ لَا

تَحْرِمْنَا أَجْرَهُ، وَلَا تُضِلَّنَا بَعْدَهُ

O Allāh forgive, our living and our dead, those present and those absent, our young and our old, our males and our females. O Allāh, whom amongst us You keep alive, then let such a life be upon Islām, and whom amongst us You take unto Yourself, then let such a death be upon faith. O Allāh, do not deprive us of his reward and do not let us stray, after him.
(Abū Dāwūd)

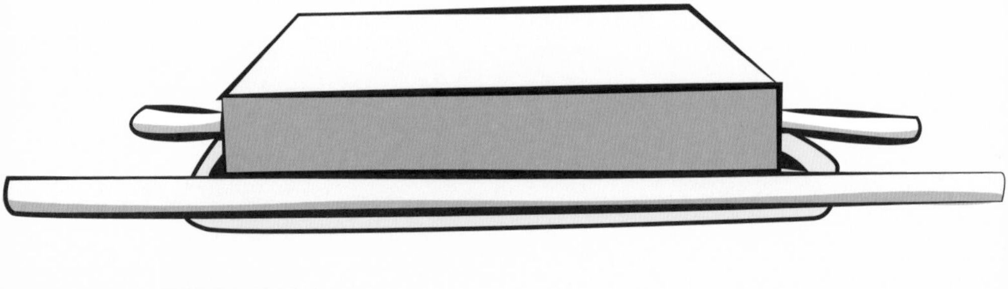

DATE: ✓ R

Janāzah du'ā' for a male infant

اَللّٰهُمَّ اجْعَلْهُ فَرَطًا وَذُخْرًا لِوَالِدَيْهِ وَشَفِيْعًا مُجَابًا

O Allāh, make him a preceding reward and a stored treasure for his parents, and an answered intercessor.

(Ad-Da'awāt al-kabīr)

DATE:	✓	R

Janāzah du'ā' for a female infant

اَللّٰهُمَّ اجْعَلْهَا فَرَطًا وَذُخْرًا لِوَالِدَيْهَا وَشَفِيْعَةً مُجَابًا

O Allāh, make her a preceding reward and a stored treasure for her parents, and an answered intercessor.

(Ad-Da'awāt al-kabīr)

DATE:	✓	R

When hearing a dog bark

أَعُوْذُ بِاللهِ مِنَ الشَّيْطَانِ الرَّجِيْمِ

I seek refuge with Allāh from Shayṭān, the outcast.
(Abū Dāwūd)

DATE:	✓	R

When drinking Zamzam water

اَللّٰهُمَّ إِنِّيْ أَسْأَلُكَ عِلْمًا نَّافِعًا وَّرِزْقًا وَّاسِعًا وَّشِفَاءً مِّنْ كُلِّ دَاءٍ

O Allāh, I ask You for beneficial knowledge, plentiful provision and cure from all diseases.
(Dāraquṭnī)

DATE:	✓	R

C5
Du'ā'

For protection against calamaties

"Whoever recites it three times in the morning will not be afflicted by any calamity before evening, and whoever recites it three times in the evening will not be overtaken by any calamity before morning."
(Abū Dāwūd)

بِسْمِ اللهِ الَّذِي لَا يَضُرُّ مَعَ اسْمِهِ شَيْءٌ فِي الْأَرْضِ وَلَا فِي

السَّمَاءِ وَهُوَ السَّمِيعُ الْعَلِيمُ

In the Name of Allāh, Who with His Name nothing can cause harm in the Earth nor in the heavens, and He is the All-Hearing, the All-Knowing. (Recite three times in Arabic).

DATE:	✓	R

Du'ā' to make on Laylatul Qadr

'Ā'ishah (رضي الله عنها) narrated: "I said: 'O Messenger of Allāh, what is your view if I know when the Night of al-Qadr is, then what should I say in it?'" He said: "Say:

اللَّهُمَّ إِنَّكَ عُفُوٌّ تُحِبُّ الْعَفْوَ فَاعْفُ عَنِّي

O Allāh, You are pardoning and You love to pardon, so pardon me. (Tirmidhī)

DATE:	✓	R

When sighting the crescent moon

اَللّٰهُمَّ أَهِلَّهُ عَلَيْنَا بِالْأَمْنِ وَالْإِيمَانِ، والسَّلَامَةِ وَالْإِسْلَامِ،

وَالتَّوْفِيقِ لِمَا تُحِبُّ وَتَرْضَى، رَبُّنَا وَرَبُّكَ اللهُ

O Allāh, let the crescent loom above us in peace and faith, safety and Islām, and in agreement with all that You love and pleases You. Our Lord and your Lord is Allāh. (Tirmidhī)

DATE:	✓	R

At the conclusion of a gathering

سُبْحَانَ اللهِ وَبِحَمْدِهِ، سُبْحَانَكَ اللّٰهُمَّ وَبِحَمْدِكَ، أَشْهَدُ أَنْ لَّا إِلٰهَ إِلَّا أَنْتَ

أَسْتَغْفِرُكَ وَأَتُوبُ إِلَيْكَ

Glory is to You, O Allāh, and praise is to You. I bear witness that none has the right to be worshipped except You. I seek Your forgiveness and turn to You in repentance. (Al Ḥākim)

DATE:	✓	R

When feeling body pain

(3 Times) بِسْمِ اللهِ

(7 Times) أَعُوذُ بِاللهِ وَقُدْرَتِهِ مِنْ شَرِّ مَا أَجِدُ وَأُحَاذِرُ

'Uthmān ibn Abul 'Āṣ ath-Thaqafī رضي الله عنه reported that he complained to the Messenger صلى الله عليه وسلم of a pain that he had felt in his body since he had become Muslim. Thereupon the Messenger صلى الله عليه وسلم said: Place your hand at the site of the pain and say: **"In the name of Allāh."** (Three times) ... **then supplicate: "I seek refuge with Allāh and His omnipotence from the evil of what I feel and that of which I am wary."** (Seven times)

(Ṣaḥīḥ Muslim)

DATE:	✓	R

When visiting the sick

لَا بَأْسَ طَهُورٌ إِنْ شَاءَ اللهُ

No harm, may it (the sickness) be a purification (for you), if Allāh wills.

(Ṣaḥīḥ al-Bukhārī)

DATE:	✓	R

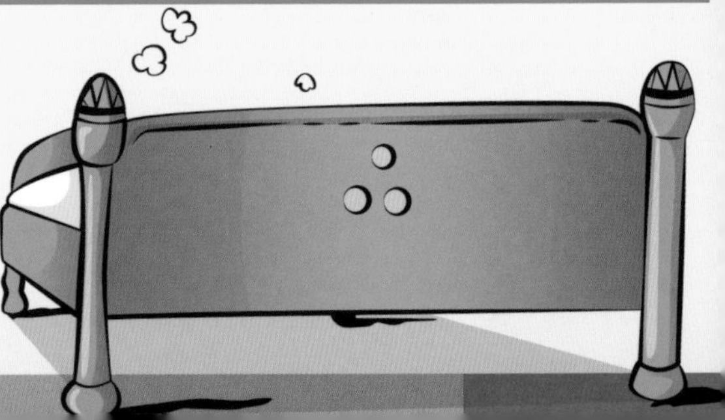

When in distress

لَا إِلٰهَ إِلَّا اللّٰهُ الْعَظِيْمُ الْحَلِيْمُ، لَا إِلٰهَ إِلَّا اللّٰهُ رَبُّ الْعَرْشِ الْعَظِيْمِ، لَا إِلٰهَ إِلَّا اللّٰهُ

رَبُّ السَّمٰوَاتِ وَرَبُّ الْأَرْضِ وَرَبُّ الْعَرْشِ الْكَرِيْمِ

None has the right to be worshipped except Allāh, The Magnificent, The Most Clement. None has the right to be worshipped except Allāh, Lord of the magnificent throne. None has the right to be worshipped except Allāh, Lord of the heavens, Lord of the Earth and Lord of the noble throne.
(Ṣaḥīḥ al-Bukhārī)

DATE: ✓ R

When feeling anger

أَعُوْذُ بِاللّٰهِ مِنَ الشَّيْطَانِ الرَّجِيْمِ

I seek refuge with Allāh from the accursed devil (Shayṭān).
(Ṣaḥīḥ al-Bukhārī)

DATE: ✓ R

Du'ā' to express happiness on Islam

رَضِيتُ بِاللّٰهِ رَبًّا، وَبِالْإِسْلَامِ دِينًا، وَبِمُحَمَّدٍ رَسُولًا

Abū Sa'īd al-Khudrī reported that the Messenger صلى الله عليه وسلم said: If anyone says:
"I am pleased with Allāh as a Lord, and Islām as a religion and Muḥammad صلى الله عليه وسلم as a Messenger"
Paradise will be his due. (Abū Dāwūd)

DATE:	✓	R

Du'ā' at the time of need (ḥājah)

لَا إِلٰهَ إِلَّا اللّٰهُ الْحَلِيْمُ الْكَرِيْمُ سُبْحَانَ اللّٰهِ رَبِّ الْعَرْشِ الْعَظِيمِ الْحَمْدُ لِلّٰهِ

رَبِّ الْعَالَمِيْنَ أَسْأَلُكَ مُوْجِبَاتِ رَحْمَتِكَ وَعَزَائِمَ مَغْفِرَتِكَ وَالْغَنِيْمَةَ

مِنْ كُلِّ بِرٍّ وَالسَّلَامَةَ مِنْ كُلِّ إِثْمٍ لَا تَدَعْ لِي ذَنْبًا إِلَّا غَفَرْتَهُ وَلَا هَمًّا إِلَّا

فَرَّجْتَهُ وَلَا حَاجَةً هِيَ لَكَ رِضًا إِلَّا قَضَيْتَهَا يَا أَرْحَمَ الرَّاحِمِيْنَ

'Abdullāh ibn Abī Awfā (رضي الله عنه) narrated that the Beloved Messenger (صلى الله عليه وسلم) said: "Whoever has a need from Allāh, or from one of the sons of Ādam, then let him perform wuḍū', performing it well, then pray two rak'āt, then praise Allāh and say ṣalāt upon the Beloved Prophet (صلى الله عليه وسلم). Then let him say:

There is none worthy of worship but Allāh the Forbearing and Generous. Perfect is Allāh, Lord of the Tremendous Throne. All praise is to Allāh, Lord of the worlds. I ask you (O Allāh) everything that leads to your mercy, and your tremendous forgiveness, enrichment in all good, and freedom from all sin. Do not leave a sin of mine (O Allāh) except that you forgive it, nor any concern except that you create for it an opening, nor any need in which there is your good pleasure except that you fulfil it, O Most Merciful!"
(Tirmidhī)

DATE: ✓ R

C6
Du'ā'

Returning from a journey

آيِبُونَ تَائِبُونَ عَابِدُونَ لِرَبِّنَا حَامِدُونَ

We return, repent, worship and praise our Lord.

(Ṣaḥīḥ Muslim)

DATE:	✓	R

Saying farewell

أَسْتَوْدِعُ اللهَ دِينَكُمْ وَأَمَانَتَكُمْ، وَخَوَاتِيمَ أَعْمَالِكُمْ

I place your religion, your faithfulness and the ends of your deeds in the trust of Allāh.

(Abū Dāwūd)

DATE:	✓	R

Wearing new clothes

اَللّٰهُمَّ لَكَ الْحَمْدُ أَنْتَ كَسَوْتَنِيهِ، أَسْأَلُكَ مِنْ خَيْرِهِ وَخَيْرِ مَا صُنِعَ لَهُ، وَأَعُوذُ بِكَ

مِنْ شَرِّهِ وَشَرِّ مَا صُنِعَ لَهُ

O Allāh, to You belongs all praise, You have clothed me with it (i.e. the garment), I ask You for the good of it and the good for which it was made, and I seek refuge with You from the evil of it and the evil for which it was made.

(Abū Dāwūd)

DATE:	✓	R

When you see someone wearing new clothes

تُبْلِي وَيُخْلِفُ اللّٰهُ تَعَالَى

May you wear it out and Allāh replace it (with another).

(Abū Dāwūd)

DATE:	✓	R

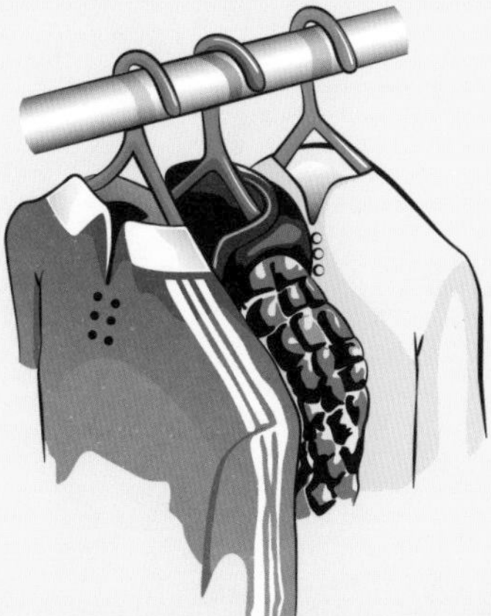

Protection from the evil eye

بِاسْمِ اللّٰهِ أَرْقِيْكَ، مِنْ كُلِّ شَيْءٍ يُؤْذِيْكَ، مِنْ شَرِّ كُلِّ نَفْسٍ أَوْ عَيْنِ حَاسِدٍ، اَللّٰهُ

يَشْفِيْكَ بِاسْمِ اللّٰهِ أَرْقِيْكَ

Abū Sa'īd رضي الله عنه reported that Jibra'īl came to the Beloved Messenger صلى الله عليه وسلم and said: "O Muḥammad, have you fallen ill?" Thereupon he replied: "Yes." He (Jibra'īl) then said:

In the Name of Allāh. I recite over you for the purpose of healing from all that troubles you, and from every harmful mischief and from the evil of the eyes of an envier. Allāh will cure you; and with the name of Allāh, I recite over you.

(Ṣaḥīḥ Muslim)

DATE:	✓	R

Sayyidul Istighfār

اَللّٰهُمَّ أَنْتَ رَبِّي لَا إِلٰهَ إِلَّا أَنْتَ، خَلَقْتَنِي وَأَنَا عَبْدُكَ، وَأَنَا عَلَى عَهْدِكَ وَوَعْدِكَ مَا

اسْتَطَعْتُ أَعُوذُ بِكَ مِنْ شَرِّ مَا صَنَعْتُ، أَبُوءُ لَكَ بِنِعْمَتِكَ عَلَيَّ وَأَبُوءُ بِذَنْبِي، فَاغْفِرْ

لِي فَإِنَّهُ لَا يَغْفِرُ الذُّنُوبَ إِلَّا أَنْتَ

The Prophet صلى الله عليه وسلم said "The master supplication (most superior way) to ask for forgiveness from Allāh is:

'O Allāh, You are my Lord, none has the right to be worshipped except You, You created me and I am Your slave and I abide to Your covenant and promise as best as I can, I seek refuge with You from the evil of which I have committed. I acknowledge Your favour upon me and I acknowledge my sin, so forgive me, for verily none can forgive sin except You.'"

The Prophet صلى الله عليه وسلم then said: "If somebody says it during the day with firm faith in it, and dies on the same day before the evening, he will be from the people of Paradise; and if somebody says it at night with firm faith in it, and dies before the morning, he will be from the people of Paradise."

DATE: | ✓ | R

(Ṣaḥīḥ Al-Bukhārī)

When in the market place

لَا إِلَٰهَ إِلَّا اللهُ وَحْدَهُ لَا شَرِيكَ لَهُ، لَهُ الْمُلْكُ وَلَهُ الْحَمْدُ، يُحْيِي وَيُمِيتُ وَهُوَ حَيٌّ لَا

يَمُوتُ، بِيَدِهِ الْخَيْرُ وَهُوَ عَلَى كُلِّ شَيْءٍ قَدِيرٌ

The Messenger صلى الله عليه وسلم said: "Whoever enters the market and says: 'There is none worthy of worship except Allāh, alone, without partner, to Him belongs all sovereignty and praise. He gives life and causes death, and He is living and does not die. In His hand is all good and He is Omnipotent over all things.'"

Allāh will wipe a million bad deeds from his record and grant him a million good deeds, and will elevate him a million degrees (of virtue) - (and will build him a house in Paradise in another narration).

(Tirmidhī)

DATE:	✓	R

When waking up at night

لَا إِلٰهَ إِلَّا اللهُ وَحْدَهُ لَا شَرِيكَ لَهُ، لَهُ الْمُلْكُ وَلَهُ الْحَمْدُ، وَهُوَ عَلَىٰ كُلِّ شَيْءٍ قَدِيرٌ

سُبْحَانَ اللهِ وَالْحَمْدُ لِلّٰهِ، وَلَا إِلٰهَ إِلَّا اللهُ وَاللهُ أَكْبَرُ، وَلَا حَوْلَ وَلَا قُوَّةَ إِلَّا بِاللهِ الْعَلِيِّ الْعَظِيمِ

رَبِّ اغْفِرْ لِي

The Prophet صلى الله عليه وسلم said: "Whoever wakes up at night and says: 'There is none worthy of worship except Allāh, alone and with no partner, to Him belongs all sovereignty and praise, and He is able to do all things; How far from imperfections Allāh is, and all praise is for Allāh, and none has the right to be worshipped except Allāh, Allāh is the greatest, and there is no power nor might except with Allāh, The Most High, The Supreme.'

and then supplicates: 'O my Lord forgive me.' will be forgiven." In another narration: "and then asks for something, he will be answered. If he then performs ablution and prays, his prayer will be accepted."

(Abū Dāwūd)

DATE:	✓	R

When having a nightmare

أَعُوذُ بِاللهِ مِنَ الشَّيْطَانِ الرَّجِيمِ

The righteous dream is from Allāh and the bad dream is from the devil, so if anyone sees something which pleases him then he should only relate it to one whom he loves.

Summary of what to do upon having a bad dream:

1. Spit on your left three times. (Spit: A form of spitting comprising mainly of air with little spittle)
2. Seek refuge with Allāh from Shayṭān and the evil of what you saw (three times).
3. Do not relate it to anyone.
4. Turn and sleep on the opposite side to which you were sleeping on previously or get up and pray if you so desire.

(Ṣaḥīḥ Al-Bukhārī)

DATE:	✓	R

When intending to enter a town or city

اَللّٰهُمَّ رَبَّ السَّمٰوَاتِ السَّبْعِ وَمَا أَظْلَلْنَ، وَرَبَّ الْأَرْضِيْنَ السَّبْعِ وَمَا أَقْلَلْنَ، وَرَبَّ

الشَّيَاطِيْنِ وَمَا أَضْلَلْنَ، وَرَبَّ الرِّيَاحِ وَمَا ذَرَيْنَ، أَسْأَلُكَ خَيْرَ هٰذِهِ الْقَرْيَةِ وَخَيْرَ أَهْلِهَا

وَخَيْرَ مَا فِيْهَا، وَأَعُوْذُ بِكَ مِنْ شَرِّهَا وَشَرِّ أَهْلِهَا وَشَرِّ مَا فِيْهَا

O Allāh, Lord of the seven heavens and all that they envelope, Lord of the seven earths and all that they carry, Lord of the devils and all whom they misguide, Lord of the winds and all whom they whisk away, I ask You for the goodness of this town, the goodness of its inhabitants and for all the goodness found within it and I seek refuge with You from the evil of this town, the evil of its inhabitants and from all the evil found within it.

(Ṭabrāni in Al Mu'jam Al Awsaṭ)

DATE:	✓	R

C7
Du'ā'

The most comprehensive du'ā'

اَللّٰهُمَّ إِنِّيْ أَسْأَلُكَ مِنْ خَيْرِ مَا سَأَلَكَ مِنْهُ نَبِيُّكَ مُحَمَّدٌ صَلَّى اللهُ عَلَيْهِ

وَسَلَّمَ، وَأَعُوْذُ بِكَ مِنْ شَرِّ مَا اسْتَعَاذَ مِنْهُ نَبِيُّكَ مُحَمَّدٌ صَلَّى اللهُ عَلَيْهِ

وَسَلَّمَ، وَأَنْتَ الْمُسْتَعَانُ وَعَلَيْكَ الْبَلَاغُ وَلَا حَوْلَ وَلَا قُوَّةَ إِلَّا بِاللهِ

Abū Umāmah رضي الله عنه narrated: "The Messenger صلى الله عليه وسلم supplicated with many supplications of which we did not preserve a thing. We said: 'O Messenger of Allāh, you supplicated with many supplications of which we did not preserve a thing.' He said: 'Should I not direct you to what will include all of that? That you say:

O Allāh! I beg of You for all the good that Your Nabi Muḥammad صلى الله عليه وسلم asked of You and I seek refuge from all the evil that Your Nabi Muḥammad صلى الله عليه وسلم sought refuge from. You alone are the one from whom help is sought. And it is upon You to answer our plea. There is no power to refrain from sins and to perform righteous deeds except from You.

(Tirmidhī)

DATE:	✓	R

When you see someone inflicted or suffering

The Messenger of Allāh صلى الله عليه وسلم said: "Whoever sees an afflicted person and says:

اَلْحَمْدُ لِلّٰهِ الَّذِىْ عَافَانِىْ مِمَّا ابْتَلَاكَ بِهِ، وَفَضَّلَنِىْ عَلٰى كَثِيْرٍ مِمَّنْ خَلَقَ

تَفْضِيْلًا

...will never by afflicted by it (this particular affliction)." Note: The Prophet صلى الله عليه وسلم would say this du'ā' without letting the afflicted person hear him, as not to hurt him.

All praise is due to Allāh who granted me safety from what He has afflicted you with and He has conferred on me special favours above a great part of His creation

(Tirmidhī)

DATE: | ✓ | R

Talbiyah

لَبَّيْكَ اللّٰهُمَّ لَبَّيْكَ، لَبَّيْكَ لَا شَرِيْكَ لَكَ لَبَّيْكَ، إِنَّ الْحَمْدَ وَالنِّعْمَةَ

لَكَ وَالْمُلْكُ، لَا شَرِيْكَ لَكَ

I present myself to you again and again O Allāh, (in response to Your call), here I am. Here I am, You have no partner, here I am. Indeed all praise, grace and sovereignty belong to You. You have no partner.

(Ṣaḥīḥ al-Bukhārī)

DATE: | ✓ | R

Takbīr of Tashrīq

اَللّٰهُ أَكْبَرُ اَللّٰهُ أَكْبَرُ لَا إِلٰهَ إِلَّا اللّٰهُ، وَاللّٰهُ أَكْبَرُ

اَللّٰهُ أَكْبَرُ وَلِلّٰهِ الْحَمْدُ

"Allāh is the greatest, Allāh is the greatest. There is none worthy of worship besides Allāh and Allāh is the greatest. Allāh is the greatest and all praises are for Allāh only."

(Muṣannaf ibn Abī Shaybah)

DATE:	✓	R

When the sun rises

اَلْحَمْدُ لِلّٰهِ الَّذِىْ أَقَالَنَا يَوْمَنَا هٰذَا وَلَمْ يُهْلِكْنَا بِذُنُوْبِنَا

All praise is for Allāh who has spared us today and has not destroyed us through our sins.

(Ṣaḥīḥ Muslim)

DATE:	✓	R

When there is excessive downpour

اَللّٰهُمَّ حَوَالَيْنَا وَلَا عَلَيْنَا، اَللّٰهُمَّ عَلَى الْآكَامِ وَالظِّرَابِ، وَبُطُوْنِ الْأَوْدِيَةِ،

وَمَنَابِتِ الشَّجَرِ

O Allāh, let the rain fall around us and not upon us, O Allāh, (let it fall) on the pastures, hills, valleys and the roots of trees.

(Ṣaḥīḥ Al-Bukhārī)

DATE:	✓	R

When you hear thunder

سُبْحَانَ الَّذِي يُسَبِّحُ الرَّعْدُ بِحَمْدِهِ، وَالْمَلَائِكَةُ مِنْ خِيفَتِهِ

How perfect is the One whose purity and praise the thunder declares, as do the angels in awe of Him.
(Muwaṭṭa)

DATE:	✓	R

When visiting the graveyard

السَّلَامُ عَلَيْكُمْ أَهْلَ الدِّيَارِ مِنَ الْمُؤْمِنِينَ وَالْمُسْلِمِينَ، وَإِنَّا إِنْ شَاءَ

اللّٰهُ بِكُمْ لَاحِقُونَ، نَسْأَلُ اللّٰهَ لَنَا وَلَكُمُ الْعَافِيَةَ

"Peace be upon you all, O inhabitants of the dwellings (i.e. the graves), amongst the believers and the Muslims. Indeed we are, Allāh willing, soon to follow (to die also), we ask Allāh for well-being for us and for you."
(Ibn Mājah)

DATE:	✓	R

At the time of burying the deceased

بِسْمِ اللهِ وَعَلٰى سُنَّةِ رَسُوْلِ اللهِ

In the name of Allāh and upon the sunnah of the Messenger of Allāh.

(Abū Dāwūd)

DATE: | ✓ | R

To benefit from knowledge

اَللّٰهُمَّ انْفَعْنِيْ بِمَا عَلَّمْتَنِيْ، وَعَلِّمْنِيْ مَا يَنْفَعُنِيْ، وَزِدْنِيْ عِلْمًا

Oh Allāh, benefit me with what You have taught me and teach me what benefits me, and increase me in knowledge.

(Tirmidhī)

DATE: | ✓ | R

At the time of death

The Prophet صلى الله عليه وسلم said, that after uttering each of the remembrances above Allāh affirms what his servant uttered. The Prophet صلى الله عليه وسلم said after mentioning the remembrance above: "whoever is blessed to utter these words at the time of death, the fire of hell shall never touch him."

(Tirmidhī)

لَا إِلٰهَ إِلَّا اللهُ وَاللهُ أَكْبَرُ

لَا إِلٰهَ إِلَّا اللهُ وَحْدَهُ

لَا إِلٰهَ إِلَّا اللهُ وَحْدَهُ لَا شَرِيكَ لَهُ

لَا إِلٰهَ إِلَّا اللهُ لَهُ الْمُلْكُ وَلَهُ الْحَمْدُ

لَا إِلٰهَ إِلَّا اللهُ وَلَا حَوْلَ وَلَا قُوَّةَ إِلَّا بِاللهِ

None has the right to be worshipped except Allāh and Allāh is the greatest.
None has the right to be worshipped except Allāh Alone
None has the right to be worshipped except Allāh, Alone without partner.
None has the right to be worshipped except Allāh, to Him belongs all sovereignty and praise.
None has the right to be worshipped except Allāh and there is no might and no power except with Allāh.

DATE:	✓	R

C8
Du'ā'

Du'ā' for seeking guidance - Istikhārah

Jābir Ibn 'Abdullāh رضي الله عنه said, "The Prophet صلى الله عليه وسلم would instruct us to pray for guidance in all of our concerns, just as he would teach us a chapter from the Qur'ān. He صلى الله عليه وسلم would say, If any of you intends to undertake a matter then let him pray two rak'āt nafl and then supplicate:"

اَللّٰهُمَّ إِنِّيْ أَسْتَخِيْرُكَ بِعِلْمِكَ، وَأَسْتَقْدِرُكَ بِقُدْرَتِكَ، وَأَسْأَلُكَ مِنْ فَضْلِكَ الْعَظِيْمِ

فَإِنَّكَ تَقْدِرُ وَلَا أَقْدِرُ، وَتَعْلَمُ وَلَا أَعْلَمُ، وَأَنْتَ عَلَّامُ الْغُيُوْبِ، اَللّٰهُمَّ إِنْ كُنْتَ تَعْلَمُ

أَنَّ هٰذَا الْأَمْرَ خَيْرٌ لِّيْ فِيْ دِيْنِيْ وَمَعَاشِيْ وَعَاقِبَةِ أَمْرِيْ، فَاقْدُرْهُ لِيْ وَيَسِّرْهُ لِيْ ثُمَّ بَارِكْ

لِيْ فِيْهِ وَإِنْ كُنْتَ تَعْلَمُ أَنَّ هٰذَا الْأَمْرَ شَرٌّ لِّيْ فِيْ دِيْنِيْ وَمَعَاشِيْ وَعَاقِبَةِ أَمْرِيْ، فَاصْرِفْهُ

عَنِّيْ وَاصْرِفْنِيْ عَنْهُ وَاقْدُرْ لِيَ الْخَيْرَ حَيْثُ كَانَ ثُمَّ أَرْضِنِيْ بِهِ

O Allāh, I seek Your counsel by Your knowledge and by Your power I seek strength and I ask You from Your immense favour, for indeed You are able while I am not and You know while I do not and You are the Knower of the unseen. O Allāh, if You know this matter (you may mention your need now) to be good for me in relation to my religion, my life, and end, then decree and facilitate it for me, and bless me with it, and if You know this matter to be ill for me in my religion, my life, and my end, then remove it from me and remove me from it, and decree for me what whatever is good wherever it may be and make me satisfied with it.

(Ṣaḥīḥ Al-Bukhārī)

DATE:	✓	R

Qunūt Nāzilah

اللّٰهُمَّ اهْدِنِيْ فِيْمَنْ هَدَيْتَ، وَعَافِنِيْ فِيْمَنْ عَافَيْتَ، وَتَوَلَّنِيْ فِيْمَنْ تَوَلَّيْتَ، وَبَارِكْ

لِيْ فِيْمَا أَعْطَيْتَ، وَقِنِيْ شَرَّ مَا قَضَيْتَ، إِنَّكَ تَقْضِيْ وَلَا يُقْضٰى عَلَيْكَ، إِنَّهُ لَا يَذِلُّ مَنْ

وَّالَيْتَ، وَلَا يَعِزُّ مَنْ عَادَيْتَ، تَبَارَكْتَ رَبَّنَا وَتَعَالَيْتَ

Qunūt Nāzilah is to be recited at times of distress and calamity.

O Allāh, guide me along with those whom You have guided, pardon me along with those whom You have pardoned, be an ally to me along with those unto whom You are an ally and bless for me that which You have bestowed, protect me from the evil You have decreed. Indeed, You decree and none can decree over You. For surely, he whom you show allegiance to is never abased and he whom You take as an enemy is never honoured and mighty. O our Lord, Blessed and Exalted are You. (Abū Dāwūd)

DATE: ✓ R

Du'ā' to remove worry and sorrow

اَللّٰهُمَّ إِنِّي عَبْدُكَ ابْنُ عَبْدِكَ ابْنُ أَمَتِكَ نَاصِيَتِي بِيَدِكَ، مَاضٍ فِيَّ حُكْمُكَ، عَدْلٌ

فِيَّ قَضَاءُكَ أَسْأَلُكَ بِكُلِّ اسْمٍ هُوَ لَكَ سَمَّيْتَ بِهِ نَفْسَكَ أَوْ أَنْزَلْتَهُ فِي كِتَابِكَ، أَوْ عَلَّمْتَهُ

أَحَدًا مِّنْ خَلْقِكَ أَوِ اسْتَأْثَرْتَ بِهِ فِي عِلْمِ الْغَيْبِ عِنْدَكَ، أَنْ تَجْعَلَ الْقُرْآنَ رَبِيْعَ

قَلْبِيْ، وَنُورَ صَدْرِيْ، وَجَلَاءَ حُزْنِيْ، وذَهَابَ هَمِّيْ

"O Allāh, I am Your slave, son of Your slave, son of Your handmaid, my forelock is in Your hand (i.e. You have total mastery over me), Your command over me is forever executed and Your decree over me is just." I ask You by every name belonging to You by which You named Yourself, or revealed in Your Book, or taught to any of Your creation, or You have preserved in the knowledge of the unseen with You, that You make the Qur'an the life of my heart and the light of my bosom, and a departure for my sorrow and a release for my anxiety.

Note: Allāh will take away the anxiety and sorrow out of the heart of him who recites this supplication, as mentioned in this ḥadith by our Beloved Prophet Muḥammad صلى الله عليه وسلم.
(Musnad Aḥmad)

DATE:	✓	R

When slaughtering an animal

بِسْمِ اللهِ وَاللهُ أَكْبَرُ

In the name of Allāh, and Allāh is the greatest.
(Ṣaḥīḥ al-Bukhārī)

DATE: | ✓ | R

Du'ā' for difficult tasks

اَللّٰهُمَّ لَا سَهْلَ إِلَّا مَا جَعَلْتَهُ سَهْلًا، وَأَنْتَ تَجْعَلُ الْحَزْنَ إِذَا شِئْتَ سَهْلًا

O Allāh, there is no ease except in that which You have made easy, and You make the difficulty, if You wish, easy.
(Ṣaḥīḥ Ibn Ḥibbān)

DATE: | ✓ | R

Asking for rain

اَللّٰهُمَّ اسْقِنَا غَيْثًا مُغِيْثًا، مَرِيْئًا مُرِيْعًا، نَافِعًا غَيْرَ ضَارٍّ، عَاجِلًا غَيْرَ اٰجِلٍ

O Allāh, send upon us helpful, wholesome and healthy rain, beneficial not harmful rain, now, not later
(Abū Dāwūd)

DATE: ✓ R

When seeing the first fruit of the season

اَللّٰهُمَّ بَارِكْ لَنَا فِيْ ثَمَرِنَا، وَبَارِكْ لَنَا

فِيْ مَدِيْنَتِنَا، وَبَارِكْ لَنَا فِيْ صَاعِنَا

وَبَارِكْ لَنَا فِيْ مُدِّنَا

O Allāh, bless our fruit for us, bless our town for us, bless our ṣā' for us and bless our mudd for us.

Note: A ṣā' is equivalent to four mudds and a mudd is equivalent to a dry measure of an average man's two palms.
(Ṣaḥīḥ Muslim)

DATE: ✓ R

Miscellaneous du'ā's from the Qur'ān

Du'ā' for knowledge

رَبِّ اشْرَحْ لِي صَدْرِي وَيَسِّرْ لِي أَمْرِي وَاحْلُلْ عُقْدَةً مِّن لِّسَانِي يَفْقَهُوا قَوْلِي

"O my Lord! Widen for me my chest (grant me self-confidence, contentment, and boldness); And ease my task for me; And make loose the knot (i.e. the defect restricting speech) from my tongue; So they may understand what I say"

(Sūrah ṬāHā)

DATE:	✓	R

Du'ā' for all

رَبِّ اغْفِرْ لِي وَلِوَالِدَيَّ وَلِمَن دَخَلَ بَيْتِيَ مُؤْمِنًا وَلِلْمُؤْمِنِينَ وَالْمُؤْمِنَاتِ وَلَا تَزِدِ

الظَّالِمِينَ إِلَّا تَبَارًا

My Lord, forgive me and my parents and whoever enters my house a believer and the believing men and believing women. And do not increase the wrongdoers except in destruction."

(Sūrah Nūḥ)

DATE:	✓	R

Protection from Jahannam

رَبَّنَا اصْرِفْ عَنَّا عَذَابَ جَهَنَّمَ إِنَّ عَذَابَهَا كَانَ غَرَامًا

إِنَّهَا سَآءَتْ

مُسْتَقَرًّا وَمُقَامًا

"Our Lord, avert from us the punishment of Jahannam (the Hell); indeed, its punishment is a persisting affliction." Indeed, it is evil as an abode.

(Sūrah Furqān)

DATE:	✓	R

Du'ā' for an obedient family

رَبَّنَا هَبْ لَنَا مِنْ أَزْوَٰجِنَا وَذُرِّيَّٰتِنَا قُرَّةَ أَعْيُنٍ وَاجْعَلْنَا لِلْمُتَّقِينَ إِمَامًا

"Our Lord, Give us, from our spouses and our children, comfort of eyes, and make us heads of the pious."

(Sūrah Furqān)

DATE:	✓	R

Du'ā' for showing gratitude

رَبِّ أَوْزِعْنِىٓ أَنْ أَشْكُرَ نِعْمَتَكَ ٱلَّتِىٓ أَنْعَمْتَ عَلَىَّ وَعَلَىٰ وَٰلِدَىَّ وَأَنْ أَعْمَلَ صَٰلِحًا

تَرْضَىٰهُ وَأَصْلِحْ لِى فِى ذُرِّيَّتِىٓ ۖ إِنِّى تُبْتُ إِلَيْكَ وَإِنِّى مِنَ ٱلْمُسْلِمِينَ

My Lord, grant me that I offer gratitude for the favour You have bestowed upon me and upon my parents, and that I do righteous deeds that You like. And set righteousness, for my sake, in my progeny. Of course, I repent to you, and truly I am one of those who submit to You.

(Sūrah Aḥqāf)

DATE: ✓ R

Du'ā' when asking for Allāh's help

لَّآ إِلَٰهَ إِلَّآ أَنتَ سُبْحَٰنَكَ إِنِّى كُنتُ مِنَ ٱلظَّٰلِمِينَ

"There is no deity worthy of worship but You, glory be to You, Indeed, I have been of the wrongdoers."

(Sūrah Anbiyā')

DATE: ✓ R

Du'ā's from the Sunnah after every ṣalāh

أَسْتَغْفِرُ اللهَ   أَسْتَغْفِرُ اللهَ   أَسْتَغْفِرُ اللهَ

I ask Allāh for forgiveness. (Muslim)

DATE: ✓ R

اَللّٰهُمَّ أَنْتَ السَّلَامُ وَمِنْكَ السَّلَامُ تَبَارَكْتَ يَا ذَا الْجَلَالِ وَالْإِكْرَامِ

O Allāh! You are the peace and peace comes from you. Blessed you are, O possessor of glory and honour. (Muslim)

DATE: ✓ R

لَا إِلٰهَ إِلَّا اللهُ، وَحْدَهُ لَا شَرِيْكَ لَهُ، لَهُ الْمُلْكُ، وَلَهُ الْحَمْدُ، وَهُوَ عَلٰى كُلِّ شَيْءٍ قَدِيْرٌ،

اللّٰهُمَّ لَا مَانِعَ لِمَا أَعْطَيْتَ، وَلَا مُعْطِيَ لِمَا مَنَعْتَ، وَلَا يَنْفَعُ ذَا الْجَدِّ مِنْكَ الْجَدُّ

None has the right to be worshipped except Allāh, alone, without any partners. To Him belongs the Kingdom and praise and He is able to do Everything.

O Allāh, none can prevent what You have bestowed and none can bestow what You have prevented, and no wealth or majesty can benefit anyone as from you is all wealth and majesty.

DATE: ✓ R

(Ṣaḥīḥ al-Bukhārī)

لَا إِلَهَ إِلَّا اللّٰهُ وَحْدَهُ لَا شَرِيْكَ لَهُ، لَهُ الْمُلْكُ وَلَهُ الْحَمْدُ وَهُوَ عَلَى كُلِّ شَيْءٍ قَدِيْرٌ

لَا حَوْلَ وَلَا قُوَّةَ إِلَّا بِاللّٰهِ، لَا إِلَهَ إِلَّا اللّٰهُ وَلَا نَعْبُدُ إِلَّا إِيَّاهُ، لَهُ النِّعْمَةُ وَلَهُ الْفَضْلُ

وَلَهُ الثَّنَاءُ الْحَسَنُ، لَا إِلَهَ إِلَّا اللّٰهُ مُخْلِصِيْنَ لَهُ الدِّيْنَ وَلَوْ كَرِهَ الْكَافِرُوْنَ

None has the right to be worshipped except Allāh, alone, without any partners. To Him belongs the Kingdom and praise and He is able to do Everything.
There is no might nor power except with Allāh. None has the right to be worshipped except Allāh and we worship none except Him. For Him is all favour, grace and glorious praise. None has the right to be worshipped except Allāh and we are sincere in faith and devotion to Him although the disbelievers detest it.
(Ṣaḥīḥ al-Bukhārī)

DATE: ✓ R

سُبْحَانَ اللّٰهِ [33] اَلْحَمْدُ لِلّٰهِ [33] اَللّٰهُ أَكْبَرُ [34]

Allāh is perfect (33 times). Praise is to Allāh (33 times). Allāh is the greatest (34 times).
(Muslim)

DATE: ✓ R

اَللّٰهُمَّ أَعِنِّيْ عَلَى ذِكْرِكَ وَشُكْرِكَ وَحُسْنِ عِبَادَتِكَ

O Allāh, assist me in remembering You, and in being grateful to You, and performing your worship in an excellent manner.
(Abū Dāwūd)

DATE: ✓ R

Recite once.

Āyah al-Kursiy
(Bayhaqī)

DATE:	✓	R

See page 168

Recite once after Ẓuhr, 'Aṣr and 'Ishā'
and three times after Fajr and Maghrib.

Sūrah al-Ikhlāṣ, Sūrah al-Falaq and Sūrah an-Nās
(Abū Dāwūd)

DATE:	✓	R

See pages 24-27

Recite 10 times after Fajr and Maghrib

لَا إِلَهَ إِلَّا اللهُ، وَحْدَهُ لَا شَرِيكَ لَهُ، لَهُ الْمُلْكُ، وَلَهُ الْحَمْدُ، وَهُوَ عَلَى كُلِّ شَيْءٍ قَدِيرٌ

None has the right to be worshipped except Allāh, alone, without any partners. To Him belongs the Kingdom and praise and He is able to do Everything.
(Tirmidhī)

DATE:	✓	R

Recite 7 times after Fajr and Maghrib

اَللّٰهُمَّ أَجِرْنِي مِنَ النَّارِ

O Allāh, save me from the Fire.
(Abū Dāwūd)

DATE:	✓	R

99 NAMES OF ALLĀH

99 Names of Allāh

اللّٰه	Allah
الرَّحْمٰنُ	The Most Gracious
الرَّحِيْمُ	The Most Merciful
الْمَلِكُ	The King
الْقُدُّوْسُ	The Holy
السَّلَامُ	The Source of Peace
الْمُؤْمِنُ	The Granter of Security
الْمُهَيْمِنُ	The Ever-Watchful
الْعَزِيْزُ	The All-Mighty
الْجَبَّارُ	The Compeller

99 Names of Allāh

اَلْمُتَكَبِّرُ	The Supremely Great
اَلْخَالِقُ	The Creator
اَلْبَارِئُ	The Originator
اَلْمُصَوِّرُ	The Fashioner
اَلْغَفَّارُ	The Most-Forgiving
اَلْقَهَّارُ	The Dominant
اَلْوَهَّابُ	The Supreme Bestower
اَلرَّزَّاقُ	The Provider
اَلْفَتَّاحُ	The Opener
اَلْعَلِيمُ	The All-Knowing

99 Names of Allāh

ٱلْقَابِضُ	The Withholder
ٱلْبَاسِطُ	The Expander
ٱلْخَافِضُ	The Lowerer
ٱلرَّافِعُ	The Exalter
ٱلْمُعِزُّ	The Bestower of Honour
ٱلْمُذِلُّ	The Abaser
ٱلسَّمِيْعُ	The All-Hearing
ٱلْبَصِيْرُ	The All-Seeing
ٱلْحَكَمُ	The Impartial Judge
ٱلْعَدْلُ	The Just

99 Names of Allāh

اللَّطِيفُ	The Subtle One
الْخَبِيرُ	The All-Aware
الْحَلِيمُ	The All-Forbearing
الْعَظِيمُ	The Magnificent One
الْغَفُورُ	The Ever-Forgiving
الشَّكُورُ	The Grateful
الْعَلِيُّ	The Most High
الْكَبِيرُ	The Great One
الْحَفِيظُ	The Guardian
الْمُقِيتُ	The Maintainer

99 Names of Allāh

الْحَسِيبُ	The Reckoner
الْجَلِيلُ	The Majestic
الْكَرِيمُ	The Generous
الرَّقِيبُ	The Ever-Watchful
الْمُجِيبُ	The Ever-Respon-sive
الْوَاسِعُ	The All-Embracing
الْحَكِيمُ	The Wise
الْوَدُودُ	The Loving
الْمَجِيدُ	The Most Glorious
الْبَاعِثُ	The Resurrector

99 Names of Allāh

Arabic	English
الشَّهِيْدُ	The Witness
الْحَقُّ	The Truth
الْوَكِيْلُ	The Disposer of Affairs
الْقَوِيُّ	The Most Strong
الْمَتِيْنُ	The Powerful
الْوَلِيُّ	The Protecting friend
الْحَمِيْدُ	The Praiseworthy
الْمُحْصِى	The Reckoner
الْمُبْدِئُ	The Originator
الْمُعِيْدُ	The Restorer

99 Names of Allāh

اَلْمُحْيِي	The Giver of Life
اَلْمُمِيتُ	The Causer of Death
اَلْحَيُّ	The Eternally Living One
اَلْقَيُّومُ	The All-Sustainer
اَلْوَاجِدُ	The All-Perceiving
اَلْمَاجِدُ	The Glorified
اَلْوَاحِدُ	The Only One
اَلأَحَدُ	The Sole One
اَلصَّمَدُ	The Eternal
اَلْقَادِرُ	The Able

99 Names of Allāh

الْمُقْتَدِرُ	The Powerful
الْمُقَدِّمُ	The Advancer
الْمُؤَخِّرُ	The Delayer
الْأَوَّلُ	The First
الْآخِرُ	The Last
الظَّاهِرُ	The Manifest
الْبَاطِنُ	The Hidden
الْوَالِي	The Governor
الْمُتَعَالِي	The Most Exalted
الْبَرُّ	The Source of All Good

99 Names of Allāh

التَّوَّابُ	The Ever-Acceptor of Repentance
الْمُنْتَقِمُ	The Avenger
الْعَفُوُّ	The Pardoner
الرَّؤُوفُ	The Most-Kind
مَالِكُ الْمُلْكِ	Owner of the Kingdom
ذُوالْجَلَالِ وَالإِكْرَامِ	The Possessor of Majesty and Honour
الْمُقْسِطُ	The Just
الْجَامِعُ	The Gatherer
الْغَنِيُّ	The All-Sufficient
الْمُغْنِي	The Enricher

99 Names of Allāh

اَلْمَانِعُ	The Preventer
الضَّارُّ	The Afflictor
النَّافِعُ	The Bestower of Benefits
النُّوْرُ	The Supreme Light
الْهَادِى	The Guide
الْبَدِيْعُ	The Originator
اَلْبَاقِي	The Ever-Lasting
الْوَارِثُ	The Inheritor
الرَّشِيْدُ	The Right Guide
الصَّبُوْرُ	The Most Patient

Revision Tracker

Book	Surah	Date	Date	Date	Date
F1 Surah	Surah Al-Fatihah				
F2 Surah	Surah An-Nas				
F2 Surah	Surah Al-Falaq				
F2 Surah	Surah Al-Ikhlas				
C1 Surah	Surah Al-Lahab				
C1 Surah	Surah An-Nasar				
C1 Surah	Surah Al-Kafirun				
C2 Surah	Surah Al-Kauthar				
C2 Surah	Surah Al-Ma'un				
C2 Surah	Surah Quraish				
C2 Surah	Surah Al-Fil				
C2 Surah	Surah Al-Humazah				
C3 Surah	Surah Al-Asr				
C3 Surah	Surah At-Takathur				
C3 Surah	Surah Al-Qari'a				
C3 Surah	Surah Al-Adiyat				
C3 Surah	Surah Az-Zalzala				

Date	Date	Date	Date	Date	Date	Date	Date

Revision Tracker

Book	Surah	Date	Date	Date	Date
C4 Surah	Surah Al-Bayyina				
C4 Surah	Surah Al-Qadr				
C4 Surah	Surah Al-Alaq				
C4 Surah	Surah At-Tin				
C5 Surah	Surah Al-Inshirah				
C5 Surah	Surah Adh-Duha				
C5 Surah	Surah Al-Layl				
C5 Surah	Surah Ash-Shams				
C5 Surah	Surah Al-Balad				
C6 Surah	Surah Al-Fajr				
C6 Surah	Surah Al-Ghashiya				
C7 Surah	Surah Yasin				
C7 Surah	Surah As-Sajdah				
C8 Surah	Surah Al-Mulk				
C8 Surah	Surah Al-Waqiyah				

Date	Date	Date	Date	Date	Date	Date	Date

Revision Tracker

	Du'ā'	Date	Date	Date	Date
F1 Du'ā'	The First Kalimah				
F1 Du'ā'	Before starting anything				
F1 Du'ā'	After completing anything				
F1 Du'ā'	When we want to do something				
F1 Du'ā'	When someone gives us something				
F1 Du'ā'	When we see something nice				
F1 Du'ā'	When we see something great				
F1 Du'ā'	When we climb up the stairs				
F1 Du'ā'	When we go down the stairs				
F1 Du'ā'	When we make a mistake				
F1 Du'ā'	Ta'awwudh				
F1 Du'ā'	At the time of eating				
F1 Du'ā'	At the time of sleeping				
F1 Du'ā'	When greeting a Muslim				
F1 Du'ā'	Reply to the salām				
F1 Du'ā'	At the time of drinking water				
F1 Du'ā'	After drinking water				
F2 Du'ā'	The Second Kalimah				
F2 Du'ā'	The Third Kalimah				
F2 Du'ā'	When we hear our Beloved Messenger صلى الله عليه وسلم's name				
F2 Du'ā'	When we lose something				
F2 Du'ā'	When we are frightened				
F2 Du'ā'	When we sneeze				
F2 Du'ā'	When another person sneezes				
F2 Du'ā'	The reply of the sneezing person				
F2 Du'ā'	When entering the washroom				

Date	Date	Date	Date	Date	Date	Date	Date

Revision Tracker

	Du'ā'	Date	Date	Date	Date
F2 Du'ā'	When leaving the washroom				
F2 Du'ā'	After eating				
F2 Du'ā'	When we forget to recite the du'ā' at the time of eating				
F2 Du'ā'	When drinking milk				
F2 Du'ā'	When waking up				
C1 Du'ā'	The Forth Kalimah				
C1 Du'ā'	The Fifth Kalimah				
C1 Du'ā'	Takbīr Taḥrīmah				
C1 Du'ā'	Du'ā' al-Istiftāḥ				
C1 Du'ā'	Tasbīḥ of rukū'				
C1 Du'ā'	Rising from rukū'				
C1 Du'ā'	In Qawmah				
C1 Du'ā'	Tasbīḥ of sajdah				
C1 Du'ā'	Between the two sajdah				
C1 Du'ā'	Completing the ṣalāh				
C1 Du'ā'	To increase knowledge				
C2 Du'ā'	The Sixth Kalimah - Imān Mujmal				
C2 Du'ā'	The Seventh Kalimah - Imān Mufaṣṣal				
C2 Du'ā'	Tashahhud				
C2 Du'ā'	Durūd Ibrāhīm				
C2 Du'ā'	After Durūd Ibrāhīm				
C2 Du'ā'	Before wuḍū'				
C2 Du'ā'	During wuḍū'				
C2 Du'ā'	After wuḍū'				
C2 Du'ā'	Entering the Masjid				
C2 Du'ā'	Leaving the Masjid				

Date	Date	Date	Date	Date	Date	Date	Date

Revision Tracker

	Du'ā'	Date	Date	Date	Date
C3 Du'ā'	When seeing another cheerful				
C3 Du'ā'	When you see someone smiling				
C3 Du'ā'	Du'ā' to make for our parents				
C3 Du'ā'	Entering a house				
C3 Du'ā'	Leaving a house				
C3 Du'ā'	Qunūt				
C3 Du'ā'	When wearing clothes				
C3 Du'ā'	When taking clothes off				
C3 Du'ā'	Du'ā' to make for the host				
C3 Du'ā'	When breaking the fast				
C3 Du'ā'	After Ifṭār				
C3 Du'ā'	When eating at someones house				
C3 Du'ā'	When travelling				
C3 Du'ā'	When it rains				
C3 Du'ā'	When looking into the mirror				
C4 Du'ā'	Āyatul Kursiy				
C4 Du'ā'	Adhān				
C4 Du'ā'	Extra words for the Fajr adhān				
C4 Du'ā'	Reply to the words of adhān				
C4 Du'ā'	After adhān				
C4 Du'ā'	Janāzah Du'ā'				
C4 Du'ā'	Janāzah Du'ā' for infants				
C4 Du'ā'	When hearing a dog bark				
C4 Du'ā'	When drinking Zamzam water				

Date	Date	Date	Date	Date	Date	Date	Date

Revision Tracker

	Du'ā'	Date	Date	Date	Date
C5 Du'ā'	For protection against calamaties				
C5 Du'ā'	Du'ā' to make on Laylatul Qadr				
C5 Du'ā'	When sighting the crescent moon				
C5 Du'ā'	At the conclusion of a gathering				
C5 Du'ā'	When feeling body pain				
C5 Du'ā'	When visitng the sick				
C5 Du'ā'	When in distress				
C5 Du'ā'	When feeling anger				
C5 Du'ā'	Du'ā' to express happiness on Islam				
C5 Du'ā'	Du'ā' at the time of need (ḥajah)				
C6 Du'ā'	Returning from a journey				
C6 Du'ā'	Saying farewell				
C6 Du'ā'	Wearing new clothes				
C6 Du'ā'	When you see someone wearing new clothes				
C6 Du'ā'	Protection from the evil eye				
C6 Du'ā'	Sayyidul Istighfār				
C6 Du'ā'	When in the market place				
C6 Du'ā'	When waking up at night				
C6 Du'ā'	When having a nightmare				
C6 Du'ā'	When intending to enter a town or city				

Date	Date	Date	Date	Date	Date	Date	Date

Revision Tracker

	Du'ā'	Date	Date	Date	Date
C7 Du'ā'	The most comprehensive du'ā'				
C7 Du'ā'	When you see someone inflicted or suffering				
C7 Du'ā'	Talbiyah				
C7 Du'ā'	Takbīr of Tashrīq				
C7 Du'ā'	When the sun rises				
C7 Du'ā'	When there is excessive downpour				
C7 Du'ā'	When you hear thunder				
C7 Du'ā'	When visiting the graveyard				
C7 Du'ā'	At the time of burying the deceased				
C7 Du'ā'	To benefit from knowledge				
C7 Du'ā'	At the time of death				
C8 Du'ā'	Du'ā' for seeking guidance - Istikhārah				
C8 Du'ā'	Qunūt Nāzilah				
C8 Du'ā'	Du'ā' to remove worry and sorrow				
C8 Du'ā'	When slaughtering an animal				
C8 Du'ā'	Du'ā' for difficult tasks				
C8 Du'ā'	Asking for rain				
C8 Du'ā'	When seeing the first fruits of the season				
C8 Du'ā'	Du'ā's from the Qur'ān and Ḥadīth				
C8 Du'ā'	Du'ā's after ṣalāh				
	99 Names of Allah				

Date	Date	Date	Date	Date	Date	Date	Date

Credits

Mawlānā Muḥammad Yaḥyā ibn Fārūq
Director

Mawlānā Muḥammad Qāsim Manjra
Project Manager

Mawlānā Harūn Makda, Mawlānā Isḥāq Boodi and Mawlānā Ẓahīr Sidat
Consultation Panel

'Irfān Chhatbar
Design & Artwork

Shakīl Zikr
Illustration

'Ābid Russell, Rachel Larson & Khadījah Vania
Editing

Bakh Sumira Sulṭān
Workbooks & Extension Activities

Media Jamshidi
Vectorisation

Rest of the team at An Nasihah Publications

May Allāh سبحانه وتعالى reward them all abundantly in this world with blessings and grant them all Jannat al-Firdaws with His everlasting pleasure in the next.

Āmīn.

Sulaiman
Ibrahim